EXPLORE OUR WORLD

SECOND EDITION • WORKBOOK

Series Editors
Joan Kang Shin and
JoAnn (Jodi) Crandall

NATIONAL GEOGRAPHIC
LEARNING

Australia • Brazil • Mexico • Singapore • United Kingdom • United States

6

EXPLORE OUR WORLD

SECOND EDITION • WORKBOOK

Unit 1

Arts Lost and Found

VOCABULARY 1

1 **Read and write.** Choose the word that best describes each list of words.

art community ~~culture~~ language traditions

1. education, laws, music, clothing, beliefs culture
2. Spanish, Arabic, Chinese, Japanese ________________
3. painting, drawing, coloring ________________
4. stores, hospitals, schools, sports teams ________________
5. cooking for holidays, singing songs, telling stories ________________

2 **Read and complete the sentences.**

future proud share weave

1. I feel good about my family. I am ________________ of my family.
2. My grandmother taught me how to ________________ fabric together and make a colorful blanket.
3. I cut my apple in half to give some to my sister. I ________________ my apple with my sister.
4. In the ________________, I hope my children and grandchildren will continue our family's traditions.

3 **Label the pictures.** Match the words to each picture.

art ~~community~~ share storytelling tourists weave

community

______

______

______

______

______

4 **Listen and write.** Write the words in the order you hear them. **TR: 1.1**

art	community	culture	future
language	proud	traditions	

1. culture
2. ______
3. ______
4. ______
5. ______
6. ______
7. ______

5 **Write.** What can you say? Use the words to write sentences.

1. future / art I think about the future of art in our country.
2. pass down / traditions ______
3. storytelling / share ______
4. tourists / weave ______
5. language / culture ______

GRAMMAR 1

Gerunds as subjects

Running		is	good exercise.
Writing		takes	time to learn.
Taking	photos	is	fun.

run + *-ing* → *running*
write + *-ing* → *writing*
take + *-ing* → *taking*

1 **Read.** Complete the sentences.

communicate ~~follow~~ keep practice search

1. Following our culture's traditions is very important!
2. ________ my grandfather's clock made my father happy.
3. ________ by telephone is harder in another language.
4. ________ for a good song to sing is exciting.
5. ________ is the best way to learn a new language.

2 **Write.** What about you? Complete each sentence about you and your friends or family.

1. Drawing ________.
2. Eating ________.
3. Watching TV ________.

3 **Complete the story.**

making painting storytelling weaving writing

The people of the Orkney Islands in Scotland have a proud culture. ________ beautiful things is important to the people. ________ is a traditional activity there, using wool from the local sheep.

Many artists live and work on the islands. ________, pottery, and making jewelry are three of the traditional activities they keep alive. Traditional stories are important, too. ________ events happen regularly. ________ stories down also helps people remember them in the future.

VOCABULARY 2

1 **Read and look.** Match each word with a picture.

embroidery
handcrafted
jewelry
pottery
sculpture

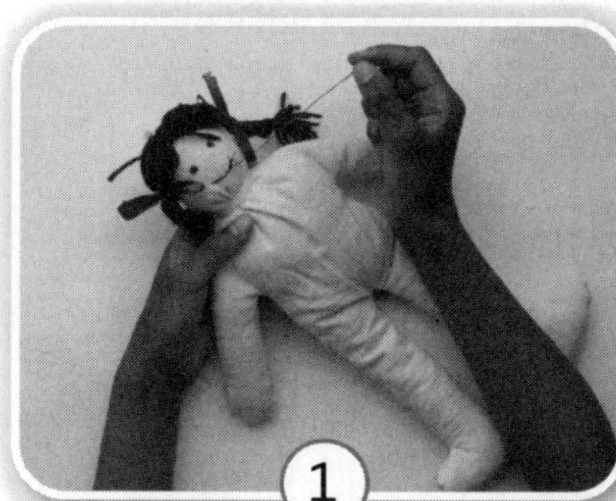
1 ______________________

2 ______________________

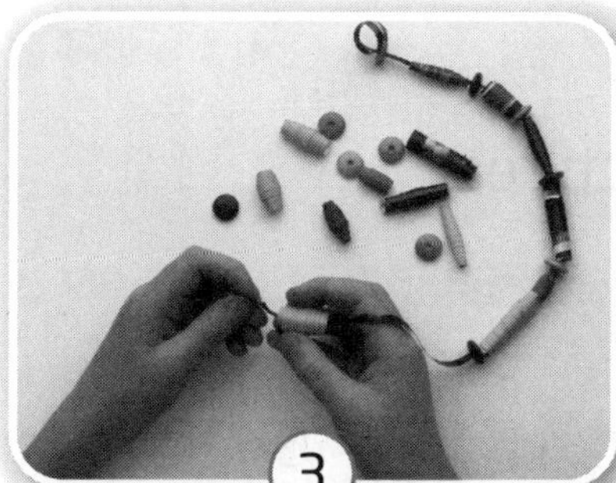
3 ______________________

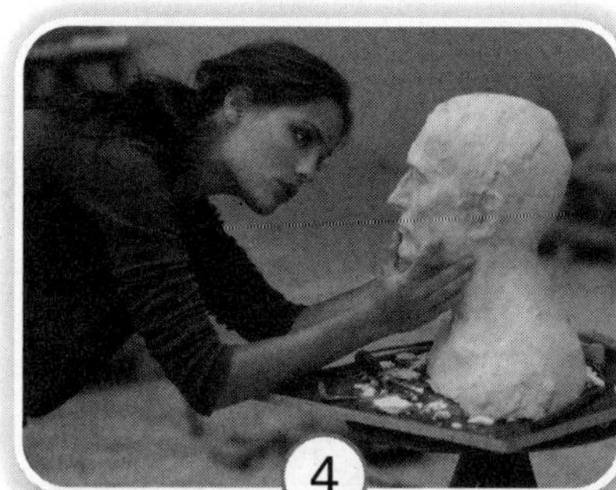
4 ______________________

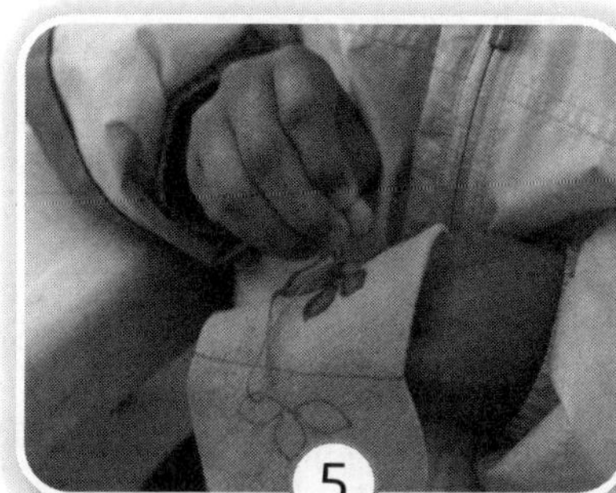
5 ______________________

2 **Read and complete.** Use words from Activity 1.

When you're traveling, try to visit a local craft market. It's very special to buy a beautiful object ______________ by a local person. Many places have their own ______________ traditions, using clay to make products such as vases and ______________ of animals or people. If you like rings and necklaces, there are many different traditions of making ______________. Or if you want something special to wear, look for clothes with colorful ______________. In some places you can even take a class in a local craft, and take home something you have made yourself!

GRAMMAR 2

Gerunds as objects

I	**like**	playing the piano.
	enjoy	cooking with my mom.
	love	

I'**m**	**good at**	playing	the piano.
She'**s**	**interested in**	learning	Japanese.
We'**re**	**excited about**	visiting	Disneyland.
They'**re**	**tired of**	studying	a lot.

verb + *-ing* word: *I **like / enjoy / love** playing the piano.*
be + **adjective** + **preposition** + *-ing* word: *I **am good at** playing the piano.*

1 **Look and write.** Write sentences about the pictures.

~~good at/hit~~	likes/play	enjoys/make
loves/swim	interested in/learn	excited about/go

She is good at hitting the ball.

SONG

1 **Listen to the song.** Use the words in the box to complete the verse. **TR: 1.2**

art	culture	family	pride	storytelling	weaving

What special ______________ does your ______________ bring to our world?

What special thing does your ______________ bring to our world?

______________? Learn to do it!

______________? Learn to tell it!

What brings your culture ______________?

2 **Listen again.** Check T for *True* and F for *False*. **TR: 1.3**

1. It isn't very important to know your history. (T) (F)
2. You don't need to keep your culture strong. (T) (F)
3. Culture can bring art to the world. (T) (F)
4. You learn to sew to do embroidery. (T) (F)

3 **Listen.** Circle the letters that make the **ch** sound you hear in **ch**ange. **TR: 1.4**

future	watch	sculpture
which	chapter	culture
choose	catch	scratch

4 **Write.** Write more words that have the **ch** sound.

Beginning	Middle	End
chair	teacher	match

READING

1 **Listen and read.** TR: 1.5

Chinese Paper Art

Paper cutting or tearing is a cultural tradition in China. For centuries, mothers have taught their daughters this beautiful art. It is used to decorate people's homes, or at celebrations such as birthdays and weddings. At Chinese New Year, *window flowers* are glued to windows.

The two main techniques used are cutting the paper using a knife or scissors, or tearing it by hand. Paper cutting is typical in the south of China. Tearing is used more in northeast China. Different parts of China have their own motifs—or pictures. These motifs can express many stories, ideas, and emotions.

It can be hard to keep these traditions alive. Some young people don't know about traditional art. But now artists are going into schools to teach children how to do paper cutting. In the future, they will be able to teach their own children.

2 **Read.** Check T for *True* and F for *False*.

1. Chinese paper art is a very old tradition. (T) (F)
2. Paper art is only used at weddings. (T) (F)
3. Paper art is the same in every part of China. (T) (F)
4. Children now learn paper art in schools. (T) (F)

3 **Write the words in the correct part of the diagram.**

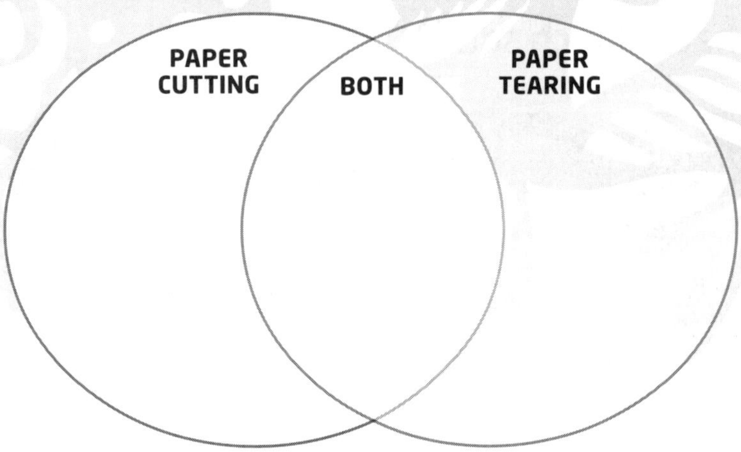

From south of China
Mothers teach daughters
Uses knife or scissors
Has different motifs
Uses hands
From northeast China

WRITING

Blog Entry

In a personal blog, you write about your thoughts. You describe what you saw, heard, or felt. A blog sounds like an informal conversation. You can imagine you are talking to your friends and use informal expressions like *awesome* and *cool*. You can ask your readers to post a response on your blog, too.

1 **Read.** What informal expressions does the writer use in her blog? Underline them.

« | » | ⊞ | Cecilia's Blog

The coolest vacation ever!!!

My family and I went to Machu Picchu in Peru. It was awesome. First, I took a long train ride with my family to Aguas Calientes. From there we took a bus to Machu Picchu. The bus went slowly up the steep mountain. (I'm really glad the bus was slow.) LOL. From the bus window, I saw llamas eating grass.

When we arrived, I was excited. It was so cool to see the ruins. My family and I climbed the stairs all the way up to the Sun Gate. It was a difficult climb. We stopped to rest a few times because I was incredibly tired. At the top, it was wonderful. We could see everything! I think my photos are fabulous. Tell me what you think.

2 **Write.** Write a blog entry about a family vacation or a special day. Describe your thoughts and feelings.

Unit 2

Amazing Plants!

VOCABULARY 1

1 **Read and write.** Do the puzzle.

attract	root
digest	stem
ground	stink
leaf	trap
light	trick

Across

1. After it turned brown, I picked the biggest ________ off the tree.
2. Plants and trees grow in the ________.
4. to smell bad
6. part of a plant that grows down into the ground
8. to draw interest

Down

1. Plants need ________ from the sun to grow.
3. Some plants, like animals, ________ meat to get their nutrition.
4. Be careful! The ________ of that rose has many sharp thorns.
5. How could that be true? It must be a(n) ________!
7. The scientist tried to ________ the animal that escaped.

2 Complete the sentences.

attract stinks trap trick

1. The smell of rotting meat will ________________ some flies.
2. Some insects look like plants to ________________ predators.
3. The sticky leaves help that plant to ________________ small bugs.
4. Animals don't want to eat that plant because it ________________.

3 **Label the picture.** Match the words to the picture.

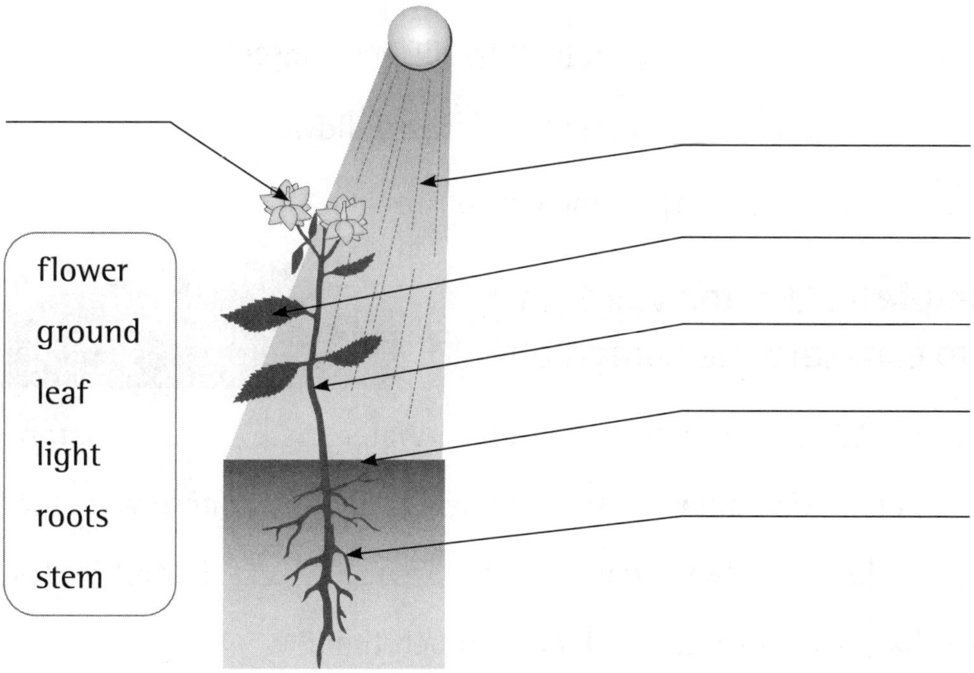

flower
ground
leaf
light
roots
stem

4 **Complete the sentences.** Choose a word pair that correctly completes each sentence.

leaves / light
stinks / trick
attract / trap
roots / ground

1. Some plants use color to ________ insects and then ________ them.
2. A plant that ________ like rotting meat can ________ flies.
3. The ________ of a plant take in ________ from the sun.
4. Plants use their ________ to get nutrients from the ________.

GRAMMAR 1

The passive: Simple present

Coffee	**is**	**grown**		in many countries.
These plants	**are**	**found**		in the desert only.
Rice	**is**	**eaten**	by	millions of people.
Bees	**are**	**attracted**	by	the bright colors.

Millions of people eat rice. = *Rice* ***is eaten*** *by millions of people.*
Not all sentences use *by: Coffee* ***is grown*** *in many countries.*

1 **Read.** Complete the sentences.

1. Some plants are cooked (*cook*) for food.
2. Flowers and leaves ________ (*eat*) by different insects.
3. The butterfly ________ (*attract*) to colorful flowers.
4. Pollen ________ (*carry*) on the legs of insects.

2 **Read and complete.** Use the words in parentheses to complete the paragraph.

Cacti plants are found (*find*) in the desert. Water ________ (*store*) in the large stem of the cactus. Any rainwater that falls ________ (*absorb*) in the roots. Cacti ________ (*grow*) in home gardens and ________ (*plant*) in desert parks. Cacti have sharp spines. Be careful, don't touch them!

3 **Read and write**. Rewrite the sentences.

1. The sun fills the room with light.
   The room is filled with light from the sun.
2. Leaves cover the stem of the plant.
   ________ with leaves.
3. The smell of the plant attracts bees.
   ________ to the smell of the plant.
4. The leaf traps the insect.
   ________ by the leaf.

VOCABULARY 2

1 Read and write.

daisy
petals
roses
thorns
vines

1. The petals of a ________________ are long and flat.
2. The stems of most roses have ________________ that hurt.
3. I'm using colorful, dry ________________ in an art project.
4. One kind of rose has ________________ that climb.
5. ________________ are famous for their smell.

2 Listen and answer the questions. TR: 2.1

1. What kind of rose has small flowers?

   ____

2. What kind of flower has thorns? Where are the thorns located?

   ____

3. What kind of smell do most roses have?

   ____

4. Where do daisies come from?

   ____

5. Where can you find daisies now?

   ____

6. What is the yellow center of the daisy?

   ____

a climbing rose

daisies

3 Check T for *True* and F for *False*.

1. Daisies don't attract many insects. (T) (F)
2. The center of a daisy is often yellow. (T) (F)
3. Some roses stand up on strong stems. (T) (F)
4. Most roses don't have thorns. (T) (F)

GRAMMAR 2

Relative clauses with *that*

I have a plant.	It kills insects.
I have a plant **that** kills insects.	
A rose has thorns.	They can hurt you.
A rose has thorns **that** can hurt you.	
The Amazon is a rain forest.	It is in South America.
The Amazon is a rain forest **that** is in South America.	
Botanists are scientists.	They study plants.
Botanists are scientists **that** study plants.	

that or *which* = things *I have a plant that / which kills insects.*
that or *who* = people *Botanists are scientists that / who study plants.*

1 Listen and match. TR: 2.2

1. I see some trees
2. I see some roses
3. I see some daisies
4. I see some leaves
5. I see some flowers
6. I can't see insects

a. that grow in a garden.
b. that stand up in the sun.
c. that live under a tree.
d. that live in the ground!
e. that fall on the ground.
f. that move in the wind.

2 **Write sentences.** Make two sentences into one sentence.

1. Plants grow in soil. Soil is found on the ground.

   Plants grow in soil that is found on the ground.

2. Some plants digest flies. Flies are trapped on the leaves of some plants.

   ____

3. Most roses have strong stems. Most rose stems are covered with thorns.

   ____

4. Some plants stink. The bad smell attracts flies.

   ____

SONG

1 **Listen to the song.** Complete each line to finish the song. **TR: 2.3**

grow root smell stem surprise survive sweet tricks

Some plants play __________ with our eyes.
They're made to give us a __________.
A plant is designed to __________.
To make new seeds, to __________ and thrive.

Leaf and __________ and flower and __________!
The __________, delicious __________ of fruit
is here and there and everywhere!
Plants are all around.

2 **Listen to the song again.** Check T for *True* and F for *False*. **TR: 2.4**

1. Trees are some of the oldest plants on Earth. Ⓣ Ⓕ
2. Only big plants are designed to survive. Ⓣ Ⓕ
3. The bright colors of plants attract bees. Ⓣ Ⓕ
4. Plants come in every shape and size. Ⓣ Ⓕ

3 **Listen.** Write the missing letters to make a sound like **al** in anim**al**. **TR: 2.5**

1. anim al
2. jung ____
3. foss ____
4. turt ____
5. litt ____
6. pet ____
7. classic ____
8. beautif ____
9. terrib ____
10. hospit ____

READING

1 Listen and read. TR: 2.6

The Flypaper Plant

butterwort plant

The butterwort is a plant that can't get enough nutrients from the ground. So what does it do? It also eats insects! The flower of the butterwort is purple. It sits on a tall stem that has no leaves. All the leaves are near the ground. They are bright green with turned-up edges. The top of the leaf is shiny. It looks watery, but it's really sticky.

When an insect lands on a leaf, it is trapped. When it tries to get away, the butterwort makes more sticky water. The edges of the leaf turn up even more to hold the sticky water. Slowly, the soft parts of the insect are digested. It's a strategy for survival that works!

2 Label the picture. Use information from Activity 1.

- bright green
- purple
- sticky
- tall
- trapped
- turned-up

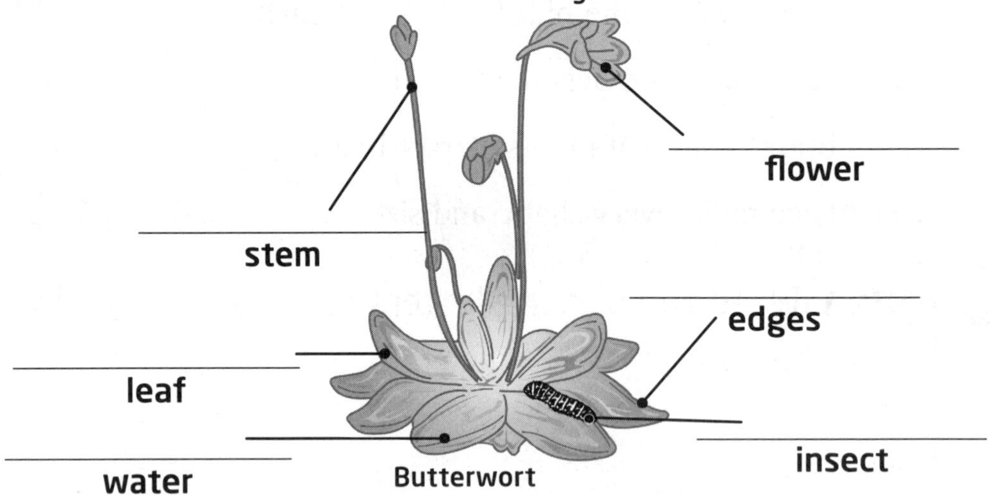

3 Read and write. Number the order of events that happen when an insect is trapped.

◯ The insect is trapped on the leaf.

◯ The soft parts of the insect are digested.

◯ More sticky water is made, and the edges of the leaf turn up.

◯ The insect lands on the leaf.

WRITING

Descriptive Writing

In descriptive writing, you describe what something looks like and what it does. You can describe the big parts first and then the small parts. Or you can go from top to bottom, or from one end to the other. Then you can describe how it works.

1 **Read.** Read about the sensitive plant. How does the writer describe it? How does the writer organize the description?

The Sensitive Plant

Did you know that some plants can move? The sensitive plant moves when you touch it. The stem has tiny white hairs, and it stands straight up. It grows to about 50 centimeters. It has many thin green leaves. Each thin leaf is made of many tiny parts. The parts are like tiny leaves. These tiny leaves grow on both sides of each leaf stem.

When you touch a leaf, the tiny leaves fold. Two by two, starting from where you touch, they close down. The leaf stem hangs down, too. It looks like it is hiding and doesn't want you to touch it. After a half hour, the plant stands up—until you touch it again!

Sensitive plant

2 **Write in your notebook.** Write about a plant you invented. Describe it. What does it look like? What does it do? Organize your description.

Unit 3

Volcanoes

VOCABULARY 1

1 **Label the diagram.** Use words from the box.

- deep
- erupt
- inside
- steam
- surface

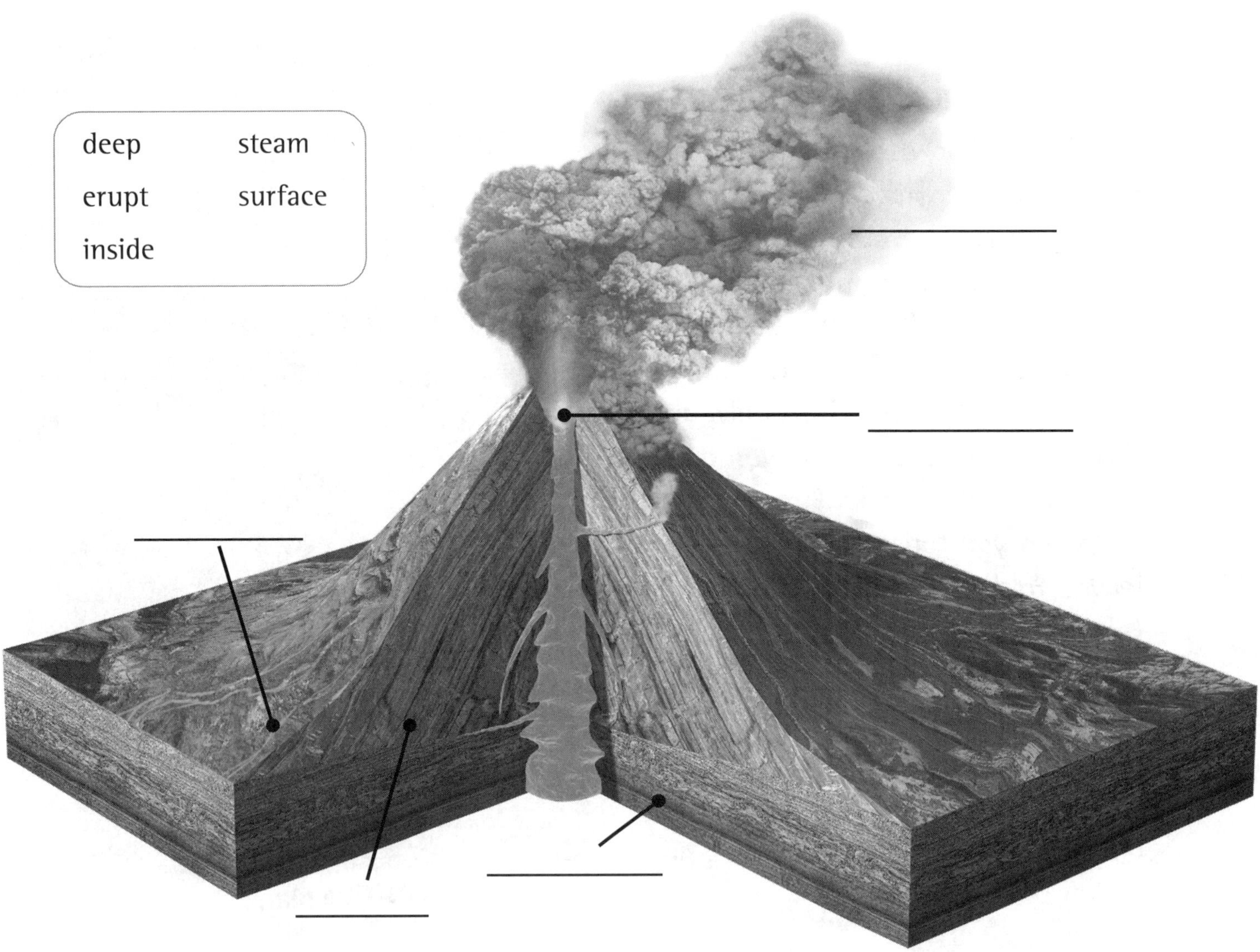

2 **Write.** Complete each sentence so that it matches the picture above it.

gas melts erupts inside

1. The volcano ________.

2. The butterfly is ________ the jar.

3. The snowman ________ in the sun.

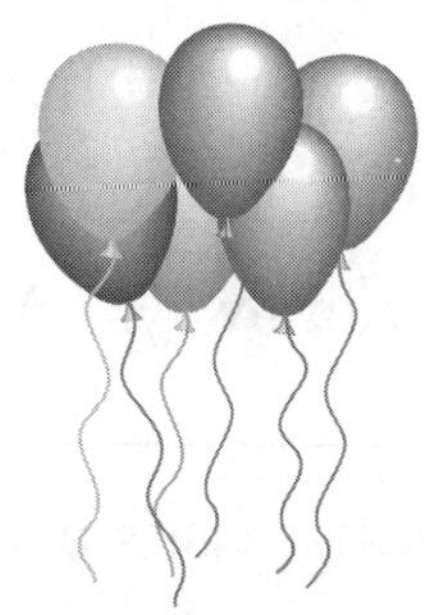

4. The balloons are filled with ________.

3 **Listen.** Check T for *True* and F for *False*. **TR: 3.1**

1. Geysers don't erupt. Ⓣ Ⓕ
2. Steam erupts from cracks on the surface of the ground. Ⓣ Ⓕ
3. The water deep inside the ground is cold. Ⓣ Ⓕ
4. The surface is covered in thick, white ash. Ⓣ Ⓕ
5. The girl likes calm vacations. Ⓣ Ⓕ

4 **Write.** What can you say? Write a sentence.

1. surface / cover / thick   The surface is covered with thick ash.
2. gas / erupt / deep   ____________________
3. heat / melt / inside   ____________________
4. steam / surface / gas   ____________________

GRAMMAR 1

First conditional

If	the bell	**rings,**	everyone	**will go**	inside.	
	the volcano	**erupts,**	we	**won't have**	school tomorrow.	*won't = will not*

These two sentences mean the same thing. In sentence 1, notice the comma.
If the bell rings, everyone will go inside.
Everyone will go inside if the bell rings.

1 **Read and write.** Combine the two sentences into one sentence.

1. I go to Goma. / I see a volcano.
   If I go to Goma, I will see a volcano.
2. The ash is hot. / It burns everything it touches.
   ____
3. Animals run away. / A volcano erupts.
   ____
4. The scientist visits a volcano. / He climbs to the top.
   ____
5. The people living near the volcano are safe. / The volcano is calm.
   ____

2 **Write.** What about you? Write sentences that say what you will do.

1. If it rains tomorrow, I will bring an umbrella.
2. If my pencil breaks, ______________________.
3. If I go to the park this weekend, ______________________.
4. If I like this book, ______________________.
5. If you come to my house, ______________________.
6. If you win the game, ______________________.
7. If I wake up early on Saturday, ______________________.
8. If you have a birthday party, ______________________.

VOCABULARY 2

1 **Read and look.** Match each sentence to one of the pictures.

1. This animal is dormant in winter.
2. This animal is active.
3. This animal is extinct.

2 **Read and write.** Complete each sentence.

active   cone   crater   dormant   extinct

1. A(n) ________________ volcano sends steam into the air.
2. When a volcano erupts, it can leave a(n) ________________ at the top.
3. Some trees are ________________ in the winter and have no leaves.
4. When no animals of a species are alive, that species is ________________.
5. Volcanoes are often shaped like a(n) ________________.

3 **Complete the table.** Write each phrase in the correct row.

Active	riding a bicycle
Dormant	
Extinct	

~~riding a bicycle~~
every dinosaur
a volcano not erupting
a language no one speaks
playing football
a volcano that will never erupt
swimming in a pool
sleeping all winter

GRAMMAR 2

Because of . . .

There was no school	**because of**	the volcano.
Airplanes could not fly		the ash.
The trees died		the heat.

You can also say: ***Because of*** *the volcano, there was no school.* Notice the comma.

1 **Look and write.** Write about the pictures.

cat / barking	hot sun / water	bike / snow
~~rain / umbrella~~	cold / open window	music / sleep

1. Because of the rain, she had an umbrella.
2. ____________________
3. ____________________
4. ____________________
5. ____________________
6. ____________________

SONG

1 **Listen to the song.** Match the phrases that are sung together. **TR: 3.2**

1. Deep inside a volcano,
2. If they have no place to go,
3. If a volcano is dormant,
4. A dormant volcano
5. If a volcano is active,

a. it's really just asleep.
b. will sleep for centuries.
c. the volcano will erupt!
d. heat and gas are building up.
e. it's very wide awake.

2 **Read and match.** Write a complete sentence from Activity 1 that describes each picture.

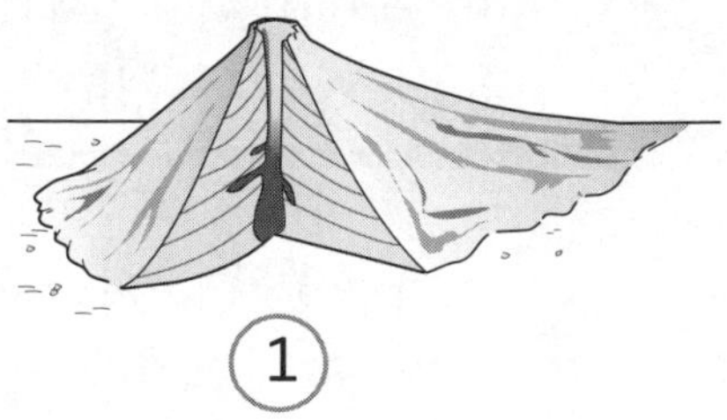
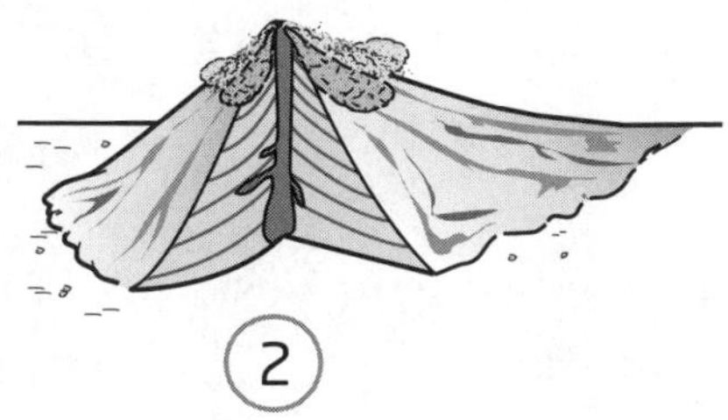
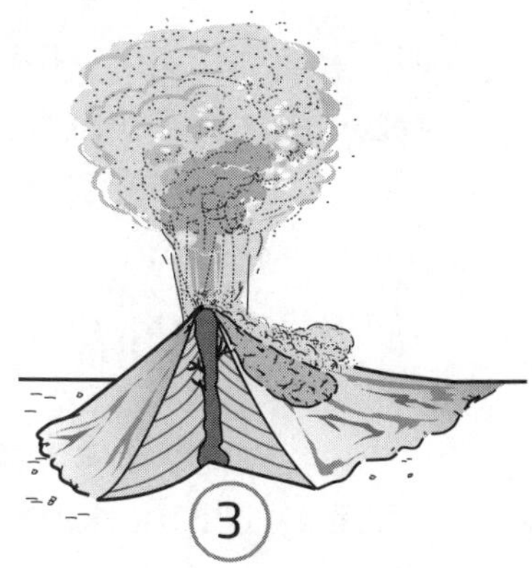

1 ______________________

2 ______________________

3 ______________________

3 **Listen to two words.** Write the missing word with the same **ee** sound you hear in the word d**ee**p. Then write a sentence using the word you wrote. **TR: 3.3**

1. dip deep
   The ocean is very deep.
2. hit ________
   ______________________.
3. lid ________
   ______________________.
4. bit ________
   ______________________.
5. fit ________
   ______________________.

READING

1 **Listen and read.** TR: 3.4

Eruptions That Changed the World!

Mount Vesuvius

Volcanoes can change the world. The island of Santorini, in Greece, is on one half of a volcano. In 1600 BCE, there was a huge eruption. The other half of the volcano broke away and disappeared. Ash from the eruption has been found as far away as Egypt. Because of the eruption, crops died, and weather changed for years.

Today, three million people live near Vesuvius in Italy. However, in 79 CE, it erupted. The sky was dark because of the eruption. Hot ash ran down the cone and burned everything in its way. In two hours, two cities were gone.

Two eruptions in Indonesia changed the world. In 1815, Tambora erupted so much gas that Europe and North America had no summer in 1816! In 1883, Krakatoa caused Earth's temperature to drop for five years. It was the biggest eruption in history. It erupted again in 2018. If there is another big eruption, where will it be?

2 **Read and write.** Complete the sentences.

1. Ash found in Egypt came from the eruption of ____________________.
2. The biggest eruption in history was ____________________.
3. Because of the eruption of ____________________, the sky was dark.
4. There was no summer in Europe and North America in 1816 because of ____________________.

3 **Complete the chart.** Use information from the reading in Activity 1.

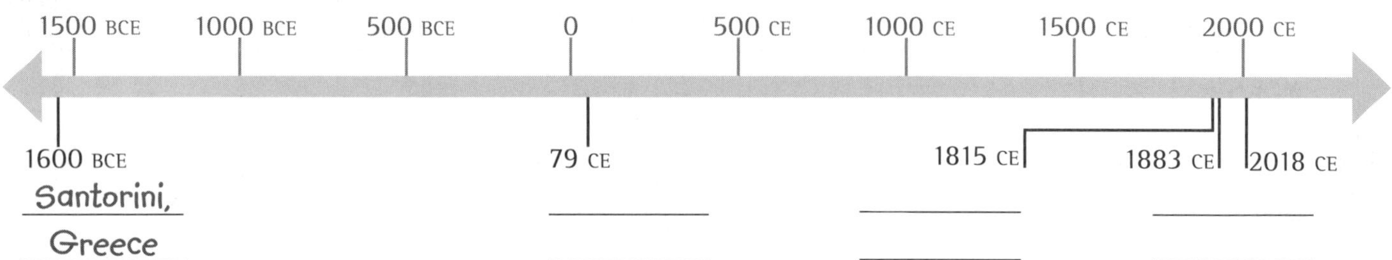

WRITING

Process Description

A process description explains what happens in a sequence. It follows a series of actions from beginning to end. Use words such as *first, then, next, after, when, while, at the same time, now, before, as long as,* and *finally.* These words show the order in which actions or stages happen.

1 **Read.** Read the paragraphs about the stages of a volcanic eruption. How does the writer show the sequence of events? Underline the words.

How a Volcano Erupts

A volcanic eruption is a process that starts inside the earth.

The big hole under the volcano is called the *magma chamber.* First, the chamber starts to fill with hot magma. At the same time, hot gases fill the chamber. When the chamber is full of gas and magma, it has to escape through the top of the volcano. So the gas and magma start to go up the cone of the volcano.

Then the volcano erupts. It throws ash high into the air. At the same time, lava flows down the sides. The volcano erupts for as long as the magma and gases push up. This can last a long time.

Finally, the volcano calms down and it stops erupting. But the process could start again at any moment!

2 **Write in your notebook.** Describe a process that you know. Explain the steps from beginning to end.

Unit 4

Reduce, Reuse, Recycle

VOCABULARY 1

1 **Label the pictures.** Use the words below to complete each sentence.

conserve	environment	natural	trash
recycle	reduce	reuse	~~throw away~~

1. Don't throw away things that you can __________.

2. You can __________ some __________ to make art.

3. It's good to use __________ products.

4. Putting trash in the ground is bad for the __________.

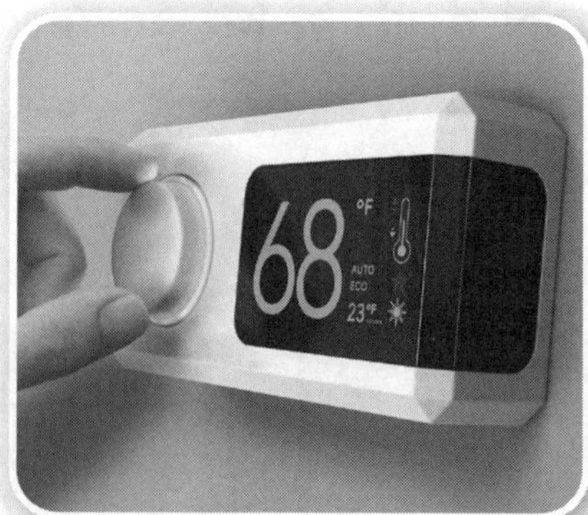

5. When you use a heater, __________ the temperature to __________ energy.

2 **Complete the sentences.** Use the words below.

build conserve environment natural trash

1. I like clothing made from cotton and other ___________ materials.
2. My father bought wood to ___________ a doghouse.
3. Modern lightbulbs can help ___________ energy.
4. Some people make art out of ___________.
5. It's important to reduce, reuse, and recycle if we want a clean ___________.

3 **Listen and write.** Answer the questions. **TR: 4.1**

1. What is the new library design good for?

   ____

2. What does Takuya hope about the new library?

   ____

3. What are the walls made of?

   ____

4. What does Natsumi do with glass?

   ____

5. What happens to glass that is thrown away?

   ____

6. What will the city reuse from the old library?

   ____

GRAMMAR 1

Passive with modals (simple present)

Most paper	**can**	**be**	**recycled.**	
Plastic bottles	**may**		**put**	in recycling bins.
The windows	**must**		**closed**	to save energy.

may = It's OK to do something. You have permission to do it.

1 **Read.** Complete the sentences. Use *can/may/must* and the verb in parentheses.

1. Houses ___can be built___ (*build*) from recycled materials.
2. New cars ________________ (*design*) to run more efficiently.
3. Energy ________________ (*conserve*) if we turn off lights we don't need.
4. If you can't reuse or recycle a plastic, it ________________ (*throw away*) in the trash.
5. Trash ________________ (*reduce*) by recycling more things.
6. Some trash ________________ (*reuse*) for other things.
7. The environment ________________ (*make*) more beautiful.
8. Some materials ________________ (*recycle*).

2 **Complete the paragraph.** Use the words below.

grow make recycle ~~use~~ wash

We use too many man-made materials. Natural materials ___must be used___ more often. They are renewable and often ________________ on farms. For example, clothing ________________ from cotton. Cotton is strong, and it feels good to wear. When it gets dirty, it ________________. When it is too old, it ________________. It is a useful and practical natural material!

VOCABULARY 2

1 **Read and look.** Match each word to one of the pictures.

cardboard	chemicals	glass
metal	tools	

1. Don't pour dangerous ________ down the sink!

2. Use the right ________ to put up a picture.

3. Use a can opener to open a ________ can.

4. Windows are made of ________.

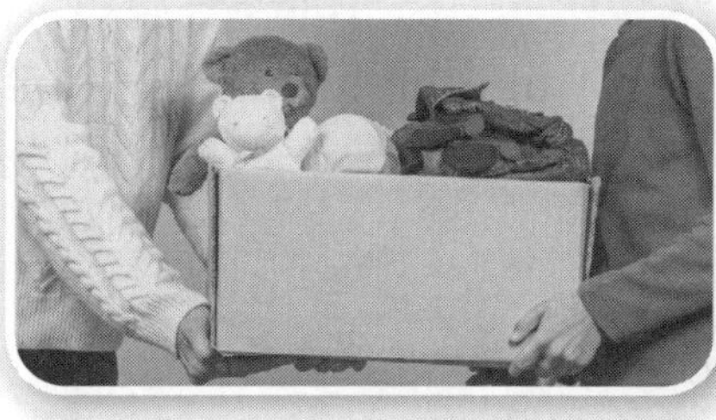

5. Store things in a ________ box.

2 **Read and match.**

1. Glass can be used
2. Metal can be made
3. Tools can be designed
4. Chemicals must be kept
5. Cardboard may be cut

a. into chains and jewelry.
b. in closed bottles or cans.
c. to make bottles.
d. with scissors.
e. to make work easier.

3 **Write.** What can be used? Use words from Activity 1.

This material can be used to make . . .

1. boxes and paper plates: ________
2. cleaning products, medicines, batteries, and toothpaste: ________
3. bottles, windows, jars, and light bulbs: ________
4. cans, cars, pots, and bikes: ________

GRAMMAR 2

Clauses with *when*

When	you reuse paper bags,	you save trees.
	I finish drinking water,	I recycle the bottle.

These two sentences mean the same thing. In sentence 1, notice the comma.
When you reuse paper bags, you save trees.
You save trees when you reuse paper bags.

1 **Look and write.** Use the words in the box.

use a glass bottle	~~buy natural things~~	turn off a light
pick up trash from the ground	build a compost bin	

1

2

3

4

5

1. When we buy natural things, ______ we are helping the environment.

2. We conserve electricity ______.

3. We may be using recycled glass ______.

4. ______ we make the environment cleaner.

5. We use a tool ______.

SONG

1 **Listen to the song.** Fill in the missing words to complete the song. **TR: 4.2**

recycling reduce reused trash

________________. Reuse. Recycle.
Do it every day.
Don't throw everything into the ________________
when clearly there's another way.

________________ is easy when you know what to do.
Glass? Paper? Metal?
These things can be ________________,
again, and again, and again!

2 **Listen to the song again.** Check T for *True* and F for *False*. **TR: 4.3**

1. You should stop and think if trash can be reused. Ⓣ Ⓕ
2. You should do your part to keep the world green. Ⓣ Ⓕ
3. Composting is hard to do. Ⓣ Ⓕ
4. Natural things can't be reused. Ⓣ Ⓕ

3 **Listen and repeat.** **TR: 4.4**

1. Help keep our world clean.
2. Don't pollute! Clearly, there's another way.
3. Recycling is important.
4. Compost your uneaten food.
5. Some things can be reused again and again.

READING

1 **Listen and read.** TR: 4.5

E-waste Recycling

What do we do with broken TVs, computers, phones, and electronic parts? They become e-waste, or electronic waste. Most e-waste is thrown away. However, the useful parts in e-waste can be recycled.

Metals and chemicals must be removed from e-waste to protect the environment. The chemicals in e-waste can be bad for the water and the earth. Electronic parts often have dangerous metals. If these metals turn into chemicals in water, they are bad for people.

E-waste often has plastic. When we burn plastic, it lets off poisonous gases. When we recycle plastic, it is safer. It takes a lot of energy to make new plastic. Recycling plastic uses only about 70 percent of the energy.

It's important to recycle e-waste and not throw it away in a landfill. We must also try to make electronic parts that use safer materials. Recycling is good, but reducing is better!

2 **Check T for *True* and F for *False*.**

1. Most e-waste is recycled. (T) (F)
2. Electronics often have dangerous metals in them. (T) (F)
3. Chemicals in e-waste can harm people. (T) (F)
4. The plastic in e-waste must be burned. (T) (F)

3 **Complete the chart.** Use information from the reading.

More electronic parts must be recycled.

- They have dangerous metals and chemicals.
  - The chemicals in e-waste can be bad for ____________.
  - ____________ are bad for people.
- They have ________ and dangerous parts.
  - ____________ uses less energy.
  - Burning plastic lets off poisonous gases.

WRITING

Biography

A biography tells about the life and work of a person. You can include key dates, such as birth date, important events, and interesting facts in the person's life. You should also explain why this person is or was important. Use expressions such as *one of the most* and *the first*.

1 **Read.** Read about David Mach. Underline the facts that you find interesting. Why do you think he is important?

David Mach

David Mach was born in Scotland in 1956. He is an artist and is famous for his big sculptures that use many different kinds of objects. He has made sculptures from sports equipment, matches, and magazines.

His first exhibition was in London in 1982. He has now had exhibitions in many cities around the world. Some of his famous sculptures are in public places. He used old phone booths to make a sculpture on a street in London. He made a train out of bricks that is in the hills in the north of England. In 2012, he made some huge, colorful sculptures called *Giants* in a small Italian town.

Some of Mach's most famous sculptures are made of metal coat hangers. Some are of wild animals, and another is of an astronaut.

David Mach's coat-hanger gorilla

2 **Write in your notebook.** Write about an important or interesting person. Include important details and dates from the person's life. Explain why he or she is important.

Review: Units 1–4

1 **Match.** Connect the words that have opposite meanings. Then label the pictures.

1. active	a. surface
2. deep	b. ice
3. steam	c. dormant

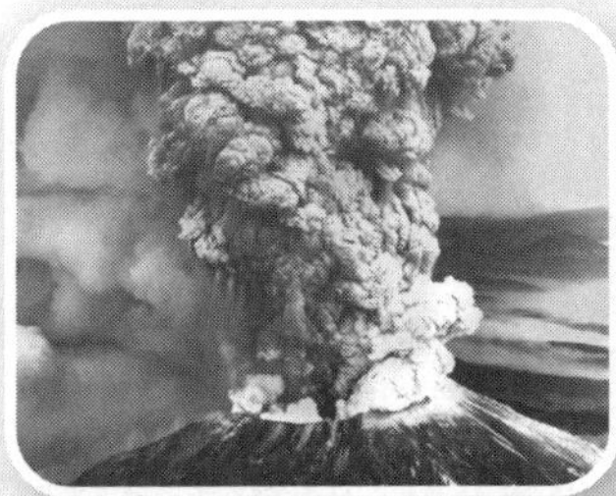

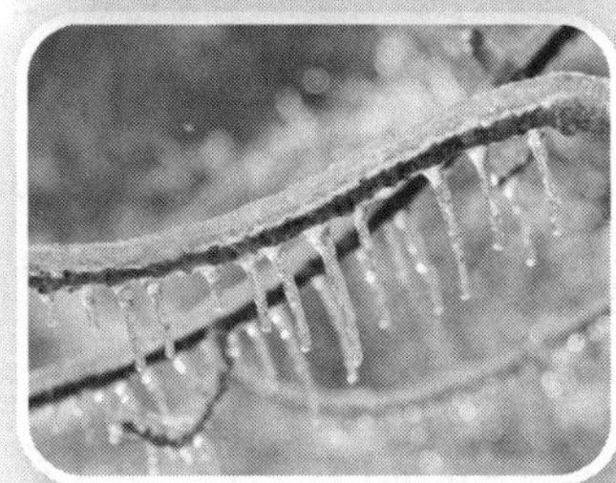

deep ______ ______ ______

2 **Read and write.** Complete the sentences.

1. If we recycle plastic, we will help conserve energy. (*conserve*)
2. If we make art, ______. (*tourists*)
3. If the water boils, ______. (*steam*)
4. If they have the tools, ______. (*build*)
5. If you eat a big dinner, ______. (*digest*)
6. If you eat ice cream on a hot day, ______. (*melt*)

3 **Write.** Complete the sentences.

1. Recycling is a process that is helpful for the environment. (*helpful/environment*)
2. We live in a community that ______. (*proud/culture*)
3. An extinct volcano is one that ______. (*no longer/erupt*)
4. Trapping insects is a way that ______. (*plants/food*)
5. Plants need light that ______. (*come/sun*)

4 **Look and listen.** Number the pictures. **TR: 4.6**

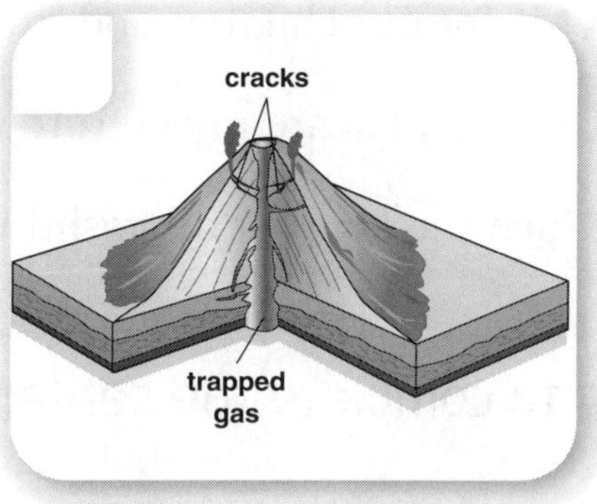

5 **Read and write.** Complete the sentences.

1. If a volcano is active, gas will escape through the cone. (*gas/escape*)
2. If tourist money can protect the environment, ______. (*animals/extinct*)
3. If a car is energy efficient, ______. (*help/environment*)
4. If people who work at a glass factory wear special clothes, ______. (*protect/heat*)
5. If bread is cooked in a hot oven, ______. (*heat/crust*)
6. If the thorns on a rose's stem are touched by people, ______. (*hurt/hands*)

6 Read and answer.

active volcano	conserve water	~~recycle plastic~~
reuse cardboard	teach language	trap food

1. We help keep the environment clean when we recycle plastic.
2. We may be in danger ______.
3. Some plants surprise us ______.
4. ______, we protect it for our children and grandchildren.
5. ______, I share my culture with others.
6. ______, I reduce the amount of trash I throw away.

7 Read and write. Choose the best word to complete the sentences correctly.

1. Telling stories is hard to do well. I like listening to stories! (*listen/tell*)
2. ______ soup on cold days can keep you warm. I also think ______ on a sweater can help you keep warm. (*put/eat*)
3. I heard you ______ with Paula. She likes ______ jokes. (*laugh/tell*)
4. ______ is the best way to stay healthy. I like ______ to the pool. (*go/swim*)
5. ______ baseball taught me how to catch a ball. ______ the ball is much harder. (*hit/play*)
6. ______ your culture keeps it alive for people in the future. I think that ______ about culture is important. (*learn/share*)

8 **Read.** Choose the correct word to complete the sentences.

1. Flowers that are brightly colored _____ insects.
   ◯ smell ◯ touch ◯ attract
2. Roses have stems that are covered in _____.
   ◯ thorns ◯ hairs ◯ petals
3. Some insects like flowers that _____.
   ◯ hide ◯ stink ◯ build
4. A Venus flytrap is a plant that _____ insects and traps them.
   ◯ protects ◯ tricks ◯ flies
5. A _____ is something that helps a plant to climb.
   ◯ daisy ◯ root ◯ vine
6. Some plants have leaves that can trap and _____ insects.
   ◯ digest ◯ heat ◯ conserve

9 **Read.** Underline the correct words.

1. A basket can be made by *embroidering / weaving* thin strips of plants.
2. It takes a long time to *digest / trap* food after you eat it.
3. People who live here speak the *tourist / language.*
4. A doctor is important to the *community / storytelling.*
5. It's important to *design / reuse* old materials instead of throwing them away.
6. I am *handcrafted / proud* of my cultural traditions.
7. We can remember the past as we build our *share / future.*
8. I think I'll go swimming today because of the *calm / thick* ocean waves.

10 **Look and listen.** Answer the questions. Check T for *True* and F for *False.* TR: 4.7

1. Because of the ash and gases in the sky, some eruptions hide light from the sun. Ⓣ Ⓕ
2. If an eruption is small, the temperature will get cooler. Ⓣ Ⓕ
3. Salma knows about Mount Pinatubo because of her reading. Ⓣ Ⓕ
4. The temperature dropped one degree Celsius because of the eruptions. Ⓣ Ⓕ
5. Scientists know about rainfall in China because of the trees they studied. Ⓣ Ⓕ

Unit 5

Exciting Sports

VOCABULARY 1

1 Find the secret message.

accident	extreme sports	kitesurfing	to crash
are	hang-gliding	length	to flip
cool	height	skiing	to land
equipment	injury	strength	to travel

1. Cross out the names of three sports.
2. Cross out four actions.
3. Cross out the nouns formed from *long, strong,* and *high.*
4. Cross out all the words with three syllables (for example, *e-quip-ment*).

Read the words that you didn't cross out. Write the message:

____

2 Look and write. Complete the sentences.

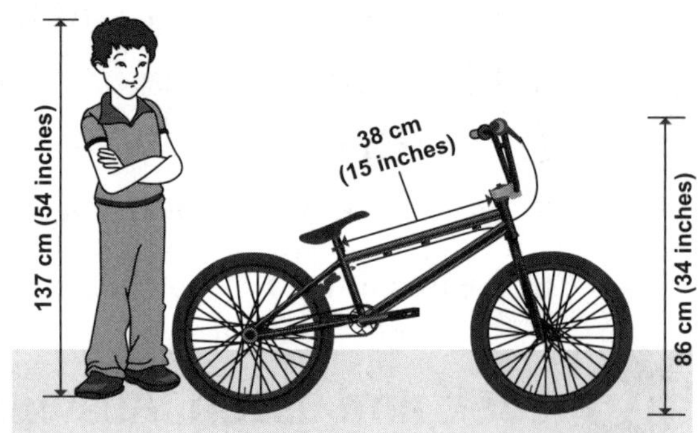

1. The ___height___ of this bike is ___86 cm (34 inches)___.
2. If you buy a BMX bike, you should always check the ______________ of the "top tube." The top tube is the bar that goes from the handlebars to the seat.
3. The ______________ of this bike's top tube is ______________.
4. The boy's ______________ is ______________. He's the tallest boy in my class.

3 **Describe the pictures.** Use the words in the box.

~~ride a motorcycle~~	~~crash~~	along the water	equipment
go hang-gliding	flip	in a field	~~injury~~
go kitesurfing	land	in the air	accident
go skiing	travel	~~into a rock~~	strength

1. He's riding his motorcycle. He's crashing into a rock. He may have an injury.
2. ______________________________
3. ______________________________
4. ______________________________

4 **Read.** Then match the questions and answers.

1. My favorite sport is surfing. What about you?
2. Have you ever had an accident while playing sports?
3. What kind of equipment do you need for swimming?
4. I love to watch extreme sports on TV. Those athletes are so amazing.
5. What's the worst injury you've ever had?

a. I agree. I like how some of them flip in the air before landing.
b. Yes, a year ago. I crashed into a rock on my bike and broke my arm.
c. I've broken a finger, but that's all. I've been very lucky!
d. Nothing expensive—just a swimsuit.
e. I like skateboarding best of all, but I'm not very good at it!

5 **Listen and speak.** Check your answers to Activity 4. Then listen and repeat. **TR: 5.1**

GRAMMAR 1

Present perfect with *for* and *since*

I've	**worked**	here	*for*	ten years.
I **haven't**	**taken**	a vacation	*since*	2016.
Snowboarding **has**	**been**	popular	*since*	the Olympics.
Skiing **hasn't**	**been**	popular	*for*	many years.

I've = I have
haven't = have not
hasn't = has not

for + a period of time *since* + a point in time
Use the present perfect for a past action that continues up to now.

1 **Read and write.** Look at the timeline. Write the sentences.

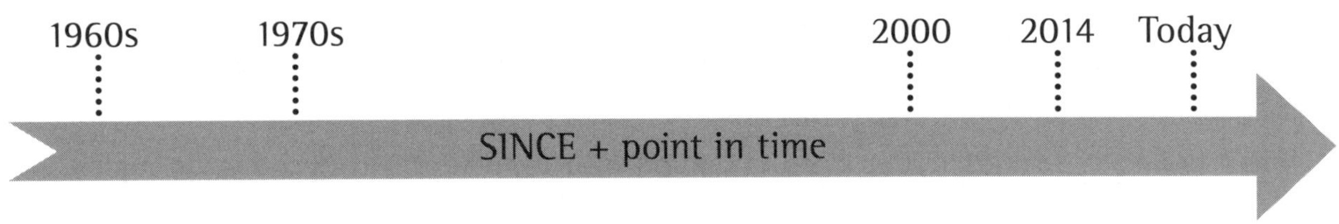

1. My friends / be / fans of hang-gliding / 2014.

   My friends have been fans of hang-gliding since 2014.

2. People / enjoy / kitesurfing / 2000.

   ____

3. Surfing / be popular / around the world / the 1970s.

   ____

4. 1960s / more than 10 million people / try / skateboarding.

   ____

2 **Read and write.** Read the sentences in Activity 1 and do the math! Rewrite the sentences.

1. My friends have been fans of hang-gliding for more than six years.
2. ______________________________
3. ______________________________
4. ______________________________

VOCABULARY 2

1 Look and find. Look at the photos. Which ones have the following equipment?

a

b

c

d

brakes	elbow pads	a helmet	knee pads	a life jacket
b, c	________	________	________	________

2 Write. Describe the pictures in Activity 1.

1. What is the boy doing to his brakes? Why are brakes so important?

   ____

2. How many people are wearing helmets? How will the helmets protect them?

   ____

3 Listen. Circle the safety equipment that Carla can borrow. **TR: 5.2**

a helmet   a life jacket   brakes   elbow pads   knee pads

4 Listen again. Complete the conversation. **TR: 5.3**

Carla: I'm going on an extreme sports course next weekend! ____

Alex: Of course you can. ____

Carla: That's a good idea. Thanks, Alex.

Alex: No problem!

Carla: Um, we're also going kitesurfing. ____________________________

Alex: ____________________________ It's brand new. I've only had it for three days!

Carla: That's OK. I understand.

GRAMMAR 2

Adverbs of emphasis

I think skiing is That sport is Those tricks look	**so / very / really** **extremely / incredibly** **super / totally**	boring / cool / dangerous. difficult / exciting / fun. scary / silly.

Use these adverbs before adjectives to make them stronger.

1 **What about you?** Write your opinions.

1. A sport that looks really dangerous:
   Skateboarding looks really dangerous!
2. A famous person who looks totally cool:
   ____
3. A school subject that is extremely difficult:
   ____
4. A relative or friend who is super funny: ______________________
   ____
5. A vacation that was very exciting: ______________________
   ____

2 **Write.** What is your favorite or least favorite thing? Why? Write five true sentences in your notebook. Use some words from the box.

book	musical group
extremely	so
extreme sport	super
incredibly	totally
movie	TV program

SONG

1 **Look and listen.** Check the sports that the singer has dreamed of doing. **TR: 5.4**

1.  ✓

2. 

3. 

4. 

5. 

6. 

2 **Write a new chorus for the song.** Make an acrostic poem!

S ______________________________

P ______________________________

O ______________________________

R ______________________________

T ______________________________

S ______________________________

3 **Listen and repeat.** Which words rhyme with **air**? Which words rhyme with **ear**? Write. **TR: 5.5**

air / ear	chair / cheer	fair / fear
hair / here	stair / steer	wear / we're

air	chair
ear	cheer

READING

1 **Listen and read.** TR: 5.6

An Extra Challenge

Extreme sports are difficult. Even with safety equipment, sports such as hang-gliding, skiing, or kitesurfing are a challenge. But to take part if you can't see or hear, for example, or if you have lost an arm or a leg—that takes courage.

Blind skiing is a sport that is super exciting for spectators, but extremely difficult for competitors. Imagine skiing downhill at 112 kilometers (70 miles) an hour—when you can't see! Blind skiers ski with a sighted skier who guides them. The two skiers travel close together. A tiny mistake can lead to a crash. Jade Etherington is a skier who has just 5 percent vision. She says, "I've had many crashes." But she has carried on skiing.

Brazilian skateboarder Felipe Nunes lost his legs in an accident at the age of six. Since then, he has worked to achieve his dream of becoming a skateboarder. Now he wins competitions. Videos of his cool moves are an internet sensation. In everyday life, he goes everywhere on his skateboard!

Brazilian disabled skateboarder Felipe Nunes

2 **Write.** Read about the two people described in Activity 1 again. Complete the chart with information about them.

Person	Sport	Difficulties they have overcome	What have they done?	What adjectives can you use to describe them?
Jade Etherington				
Felipe Nunes				

WRITING

Biography

A biography describes the life of another person. You can make your biography more interesting if you connect the dates and events in that person's life. Words you can use to link the dates and events include: *after (that), before, since then, the next year, then, at the time, suddenly,* and *afterward.*

1 **Read.** Read the biography. Underline the expressions that are used to link the events.

High Climber

Before the age of nine, Matt Moniz enjoyed summer vacations like most kids do. Then his life suddenly changed in 2007. Matt's father invited him to join a climb to Mount Everest. At the time, Matt did not know what to expect, but he said afterward that he had "the best time of his life." Since then, there has been no stopping him. The next year, he climbed two of the world's highest mountains: Africa's Kilimanjaro and Russia's Elbrus.

In 2015, while climbing Mt. Everest, an earthquake struck and caused an avalanche. Matt hid behind a big rock as the avalanche hit his camp. He received the Boy Scouts of America's highest award for lifesaving after helping rescue injured climbers on that day. After that, Matt stayed in Nepal for a month to help rebuild schools and homes in the area. He loves the outdoors and often talks to other kids about spending more time outdoors.

2 **Write in your notebook.** Write a short biography about someone who has an exciting job, does an exciting sport, or has traveled to exciting places. Remember to link the events and dates with connecting expressions.

Unit 6

History's a Mystery

VOCABULARY 1

1 Do the puzzle. Unscramble the letters to the secret message.

Scrambled	Answer boxes (numbered letters)
DEID	d i e d (5)
DUIBER	_ _ _ _ _ _ (11, 4, 20)
VEHSETI	_ _ _ _ _ _ _ (12, 14, 21)
TEUTAS	_ _ _ _ _ _ (8, 15)
OLGD	_ _ _ _ (7, 1)
MYMMU	_ _ _ _ _ (22)
NAERL	_ _ _ _ _ (6)
REPVRSEE	_ _ _ _ _ _ _ _ (16, 18, 2)
MOTB	_ _ _ _ (19)
TEACAVXE	_ _ _ _ _ _ _ _ (3, 17)
CEOBTJ	_ _ _ _ _ _ (10, 9, 13)

buried	object
~~died~~	preserve
excavate	statue
gold	thieves
learn	tomb
mummy	

_ _ _ _ N _ _ _ (1 2 3 4 N 5 6 7) _ _ _ _ _ (8 9 10 11 12) _ _ _ (13 14 15) _ _ _ _ (16 17 18 19) _ _ (20 21) F _ N (22) !

2 Label the pictures.

1. objects

2. ____________________

3. ____________________

4. ____________________

5. ____________________

6. ____________________

3 **Listen.** Check the words in Activity 2 that you hear. **TR: 6.1**

4 **Look at the timeline.** Answer the questions.

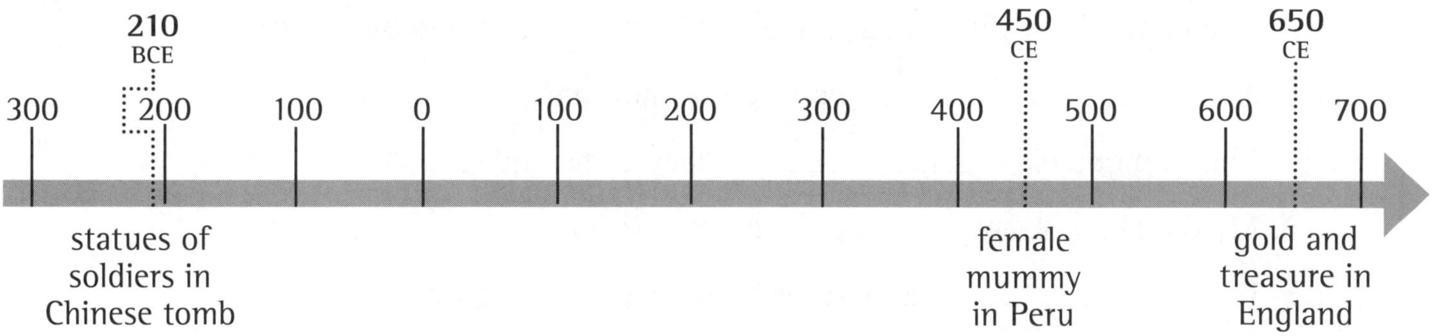

1. Which event took place before the common era (BCE)?

____

2. Which event occurred first in the common era (CE)?

____

GRAMMAR 1

Passive voice: Simple past

I / He / She	**was**	**(not)**	**sent**	to bed.	*was not = wasn't* *were not = weren't*
It			**discovered**	in a hole.	
We / They	**were**	**(not)**	**given**	homework.	

Question					**Answer**
When	**were**	you	**born?**		In 2010.
	Were	they	**given**	any homework?	Yes, they were. / No, they weren't.
	Was	it	**discovered**	near here?	Yes, it was. / No, it wasn't.

When you don't know who is doing the action, use the passive voice.

1 **Look and write.** Complete the sentences.

be born	~~bury~~
call	find
give	hide

1. The coins <u>were buried</u> in a hole in the ground.
   The police think they ________________ many years ago by thieves.
2. A cat ________________ up a tree this morning.
   The firefighters ________________. They came and saved it.
3. My daughter ________________ on my birthday.
   I ________________ the best birthday present in the world: a daughter!

2 **Write.** What about you? Make five questions. Then answer with true sentences in your notebook.

1. When <u>were</u> you <u>born</u>? (*be born*)
2. ________ you ________ something cute when you were a kid? (*call*)
3. As a child, ________ you ________ a special gift that you still have? (*give*)
4. ________ you ever ________ to bed early because you were naughty? (*send*)

VOCABULARY 2

1 **Write.** Complete the definitions with words from the box.

analyze	an artifact	a DNA test	a sample	a site

1. __________ is a place that archaeologists want to excavate or explore.
2. __________ is an object found at the site. It is not a living thing. It was made by someone.
3. __________ is a way to discover what is in the body's cells. It can help you find your relatives.
4. Scientists __________ the objects they find to learn how old the objects are.
5. __________ is a small amount of something, such as food, that someone studies.

2 **Listen and write.** How do we know so much about the Iceman? Listen to the archaeologist. Use the words from Activity 1. **TR: 6.2**

1. The Iceman was quite rich. __________
2. His last meal was cereal and meat. __________
3. He climbed the mountain before he died. __________
4. We can study what's left behind to learn about someone from the past. __________
5. We can create a picture of what the Iceman might have looked like. __________

GRAMMAR 2

Passive voice: Simple past with *by* + agent

The treasure	**was**	**stolen**	**by**	thieves.
The objects	**were**	**analyzed**	**by**	a scientist.

	Was	your tattoo	**done**	**by**	an artist?
	Were	those statues	**discovered**	**by**	archaeologists?
Who	**was**	the Iceman	**found**	**by?**	

When you know who is doing the action, add it to the passive with *by* + the agent (person doing the action).

1 **Read and write.** Use the words in parentheses and *by* if needed.

Around 246 BCE, about 700,000 men __were hired by__ (*hire*) the Chinese emperor Qin Shihuang to make an army of men. He wanted the army to protect him after he died. For nearly forty years, thousands of statues __________ (*make*) the men. When the ruler died in 210 BCE, the statues __________ (*bury*) with him in a tomb. This incredible treasure __________ (*forget*) for centuries, but in 1974 it __________ (*find*) Chinese farmers! When the site __________ (*excavate*) archaeologists a few years later, more than 6,000 statues __________ (*discover*). There were soldiers, horses, musicians, and acrobats! Originally, the statues __________ (*paint*) in different colors, but now the colors have gone. All the same, they are beautiful because each statue is different! Can you see the differences?

SONG

1 **Listen to the song.** Number the words in the order that you first hear them (1–5). **TR: 6.3**

a. scientists

b. mummies

c. money

d. pottery

e. statues

2 **Listen.** Circle the words that have the same sound as **augh** in the word t**augh**t. Then underline the letters in the words that make the sound. **TR: 6.4**

taught	drought	saw	frown
knew	bought	course	astronaut
fought	caught	sew	draw

READING

1 Listen and read. TR: 6.5

Trash Is Treasure

All archaeologists study human history, but there are many kinds of archaeologists. Forensic archaeologists analyze DNA and help police with crimes. Landscape archaeologists study sites. Osteologists are interested in bones. And there are "garbologists" who study trash.

Garbology is an important part of archaeology. To learn more about the population of some ancient civilizations, archaeologists study the trash that is left behind. These remains can show us what objects people threw away, as well as what food they ate and diseases they had.

Weird but true **Archaeologists studying trash discovered in Herculaneum found lost jewelry, coins, and semi-precious stones!**

Surprisingly, a lot of the trash from the past is still useful today. Archaeologists have discovered that biodegradable trash buried underground does not decompose as quickly as we thought. We can learn about human history from what people threw away. Would you like to be a garbologist?

2 Check T for *True* and F for *False*.

1. Not all archaeologists work at ancient sites. (T) (F)
2. The trash buried underground can't help us learn about the past. (T) (F)
3. Biodegradable trash decomposes quickly when it is buried. (T) (F)

3 **Read again.** Label the tree. What does each kind of archaeologist study?

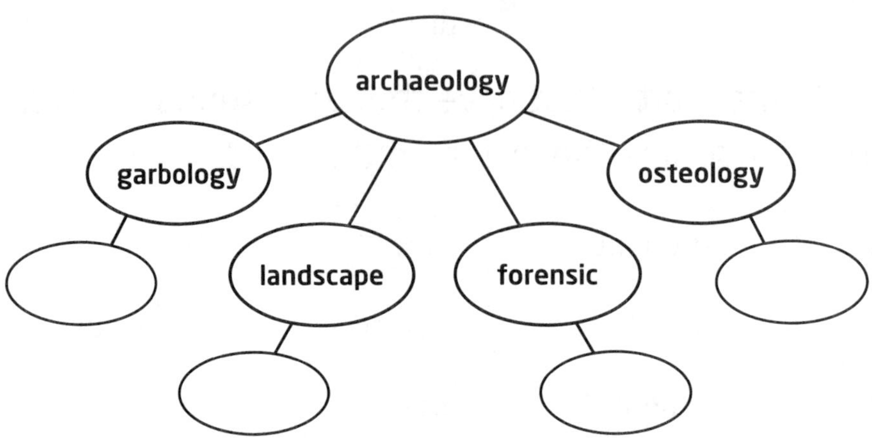

WRITING

Exemplification Writing

In this type of writing, you give examples that support important ideas in your text. Be clear and show the reader that you know what you are writing about. To do this, add examples of facts. Use expressions like: *for instance, such as, namely, specifically,* and *a good example is.* These words let the reader know that more information is coming in the text.

1 **Read.** Underline all the expressions that refer to examples.

Memories from the Past

Archaeologists feel very excited when new discoveries are made because each new discovery tells them more about the past. A good example is the famous Iceman mummy discovered in 1991 by hikers in the Alps.

Thanks to DNA tests, CT scans, and artifacts found near the site, we know more about people who lived long ago, namely, what they wore and how they lived. The Iceman tells us a lot.

So does the famous Peruvian female mummy. For instance, we know that she was probably 12 to 14 years old when she died. She was in very good health. Specifically, she had very strong bones and great teeth.

Although we still don't know everything about these mummies, the Iceman and the Peruvian mummy are two incredible discoveries that tell us more about the past.

2 **Write in your notebook.** Write about the terra-cotta statues. What does this discovery tell us about the past? Use examples.

Unit 7

Chocolate!

VOCABULARY 1

1 **Read and write.** Complete the sentences. Then do the puzzle.

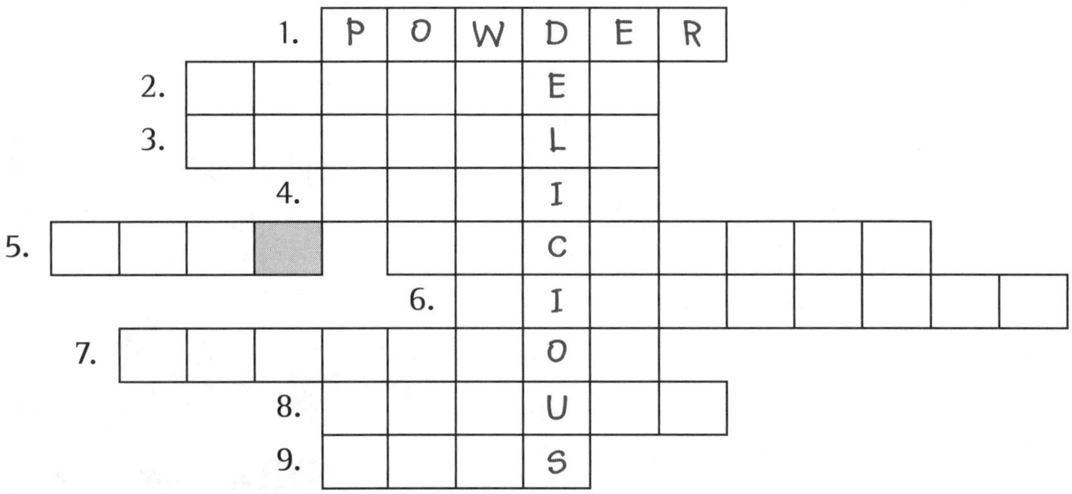

1. Cocoa _____powder_____ is dry, but you can drink it if you add hot milk.
2. ____________________ and strawberries go well with chocolate.
3. I think that ________________ is a boring flavor, but it tastes good in ice cream.
4. The opposite of liquid is ____________________________.
5. I like to mix chocolate and milk and drink __________________ on cold days.
6. You can use ice cream and milk to make a ________________________.
7. This spice smells nice. It's brown and it's called __________________.
8. People learned how to change chocolate from ____________________ to solid.
9. Cacao ____________________ contain many seeds. One has enough for seven candy bars!

2 **Read and write.** Which word doesn't belong? Underline the "odd word out." Then use the underlined words to label the photos below.

1. milkshake	vanilla	hot chocolate	candy bar
2. cinnamon	solid	sugar	spices
3. solid	liquid	powder	caramel
4. pods	vanilla	cinnamon	sugar

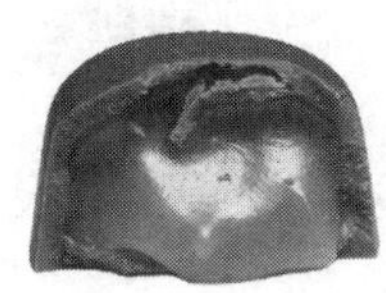

3 **Look at the photos and write the questions.**
Then write your answers.

1. What / your / favorite type?

______________________________ ______________

2. How many / you / eat / every week?

______________________________ ______________

3. you / ever / drink?

______________________________ ______________

4. you / know / how to make?

______________________________ ______________

GRAMMAR 1

Past progressive

I / He / She	**was**	**studying.**	
We / They	**were**	**taking**	a test.

Question					Answer
Where	**was**	she	**going?**		She was going to the store.
What	**were**	you	**doing**	last night?	I was playing video games.

Use the past progressive for actions in progress in the past.

1 **Write.** Write the *-ing* form of the verbs.

1. eat ___________
2. live ___________
3. win ___________
4. make ___________
5. swim ___________
6. sleep ___________

2 **Complete the sentences.** Then listen and check your answers. **TR: 7.1**

Mom: What were you doing (*you / do*) last night, Sarah?

Sarah: What do you mean, Mom? I ___________ (*sleep*)!

Dad: No, you ___________ (*not sleep*). I heard you. You ___________ (*walk*) around the house at 3 A.M.

Thomas: I heard her, too, Dad. She ___________ (*make*) a noise in the kitchen.

Mom: I don't understand. Why ___________ (*you / make*) a noise downstairs, Sarah?

Sarah: I ___________ (*make*) a . . . CAKE! Happy birthday, Mom!

3 **Write.** What about you? Write what you were doing at these times.

1. At 8 P.M. last night, I ___________________________.
2. Half an hour ago, I ___________________________.
3. I ___________________________ when the cell phone rang.
4. When I injured myself, I ___________________________.

VOCABULARY 2

1 **Listen.** Listen to the story. Number the words in the order you hear them. **TR: 7.2**

◯ teaspoons ◯ ingredients ◯ mix (1) recipe ◯ pour

2 **Listen to the rest of the story.** Circle the correct answers. **TR: 7.3**

1. What are they making?
   a. chocolate ice cream b. a chocolate milkshake
2. Why can't they pour it?
   a. It's too thick. b. They can't find the glasses.
3. What was the mistake?
   a. They didn't mix it enough. b. They didn't add enough milk.

3 **Match the questions and answers.**

1. I really want to drink this chocolate milkshake! How about you?
2. Where's the recipe?
3. So, do we have all the ingredients?
4. How many teaspoons of cocoa powder should I put in?
5. Should I pour it now?

a. Six is fine. Then mix it with the ice cream and the milk.
b. Me too. I haven't had one for months!
c. It's here. I put it in front of us so we can see it.
d. Sure. Here are the glasses.
e. I think so. We have milk, ice cream, and cocoa powder.

4 **Read the banana milkshake recipe**. Underline the correct words.

Print the *menu* / *recipe* for the banana milkshake. Check that you have all the *ingredients* / *pods*. Put the milk, ice cream, banana, and a *powder* / *teaspoon* of sugar in the blender. Mix everything together for one minute. Pour the *solid* / *liquid* into two glasses.

GRAMMAR 2

Cause and effect with simple past and modals

Wei-Wei **put** the recipe in front of her	**so that**	she	**could**	see it.
She **turned on** the oven		it	**would**	be ready.
She **put** a lid on the bowl		it	**wouldn't**	spill.

Use *so that* to explain the reason for an action.

1 Complete the sentences.

1. I printed out the recipe so that we ___could read___ it before we cooked. (*can / read*)
2. We put some cinnamon on the banana milkshake so that it ________________ more interesting. (*will / taste*)
3. We used a blender so that we ________________ the ingredients more quickly. (*can / mix*)
4. I did my homework in the afternoon so that I ________________ later. (*can / watch TV*)
5. Sarah hid the cake so that her mom ________________ it. (*will not / see*)

2 Match the cause and effect.

a saucer

a coffee house

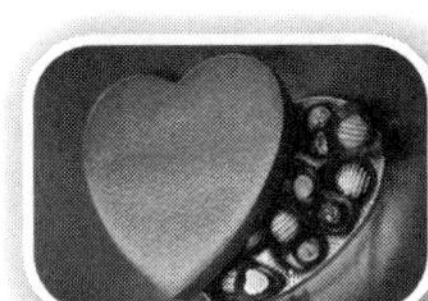
a box of candy

a wrapper

brownies

1. Saucers were invented
2. Coffee houses were built
3. Candy boxes were made
4. Candy wrappers were used
5. Brownie recipes were published in magazines

a. so that hot liquids wouldn't fall on clothes.
b. so that we could send chocolate to people we love.
c. so that people could make brownies at home.
d. so that the chocolate wouldn't get dirty.
e. so that people could meet to have a drink and talk.

SONG

1 **Match the words and the pictures.**

a cup heat it up pour spice sprinkle stir

a. pour

b. ______

c. ______

d. ______

e. ______

f. ______

2 **Listen to the song.** As you listen, number the order (1-6) that you hear the words in Activity 1. **TR: 7.4**

3 **Listen and repeat.** Write the missing letters that sound like **ng** in eati**ng**. Then write more words that have the same **ng** sound. **TR: 7.5**

1. eati ng
2. stro ______
3. le ______ th
4. runni ______
5. maki ______
6. exciti ______
7. stre ______ th
8. ha ______-glidi ______

____

____

READING

1 Listen and read. **TR: 7.6**

The Sweet World of Art

Italian Mirco Della Vecchia, born in 1980, is both a chef and an artist. He has won many prizes for his awesome ice creams and chocolate cakes. From 1994 until 2000, he worked in famous chocolate stores in Italy and Switzerland. In 2000, he opened his first chocolate store. Today, he has cafés all over the world, which are popular for coffee and ice cream. His ice cream is made from fresh milk, cocoa from Venezuela, Colombian coffee, and nuts from Italy.

In 2011, Vecchia organized the World Chocolate Exhibition. Together with other artists, Vecchia carefully built miniature reproductions of famous sites around the world . . . in chocolate! In 2012, Vecchia made the largest chocolate sculpture in the world! It is over 4 meters tall and took one month to freeze! How does he make the sculptures without eating them? Amazing!

2 Read the text again. Complete the timeline.

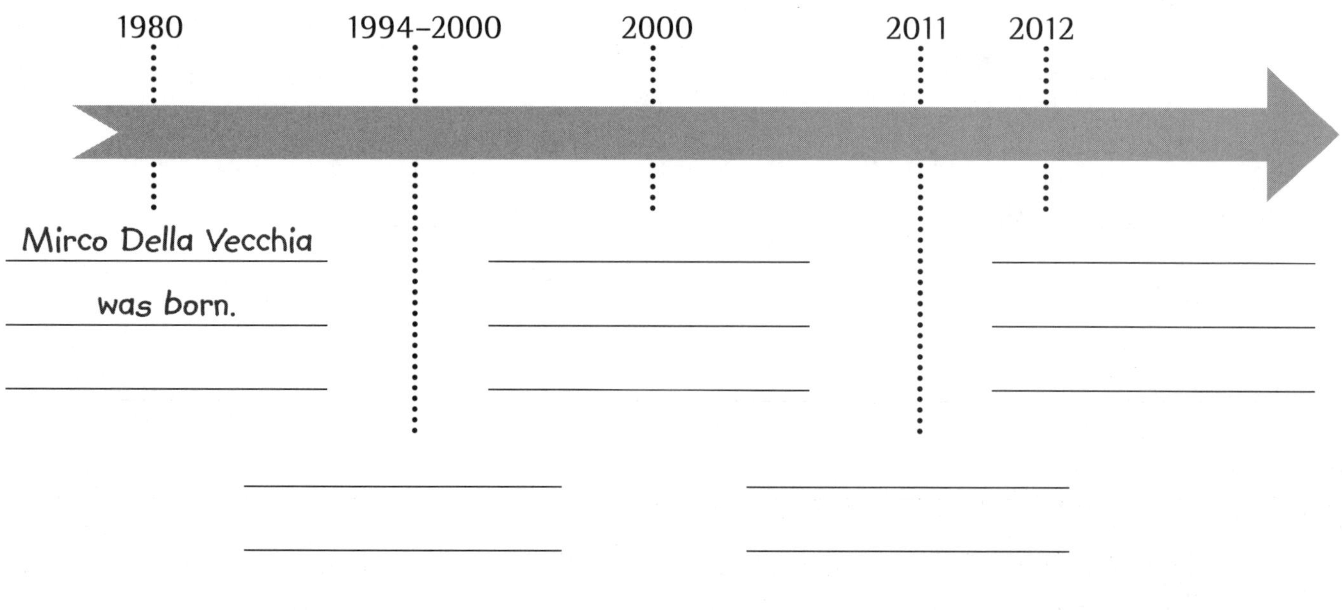

WRITING

Paragraph Unity

A good paragraph has unity—all the sentences in the paragraph refer to and explain the main idea. The topic sentence expresses the main idea, and the supporting sentences give related details that extend the main idea. When you write a paragraph, check to make sure all the sentences are closely related to the topic.

1 **Read.** Cross out three sentences in each blog response that do not belong.

« | » | ⊞ |

Chocolate Customs

Keiko, Osaka In my country, Japan, chocolate is very popular. Valentine's Day is a big deal in my country. The history of chocolate is interesting. Unlike most countries, however, on Valentine's Day, only women give chocolate to men! International Chocolate Day is in September. But women get chocolate, too. On March 14, or White Day, men give chocolates to women. It all works out in the end, with everyone eating plenty of chocolate in February and March. Our school year starts in April.

Pablo, Mexico City In my family we use chocolate on Day of the Dead, a Mexican holiday in early November. The cacao tree comes from Mexico. Mexico City is the capital of Mexico. Our ancestors would be surprised to see how the little cacao bean has evolved. Today there are more than 40,000 types of chocolate candy bars. Most supermarkets are open until 9PM. Despite the variety of chocolate, our family uses it in just two ways. First, my mom cooks a meal with chocolate sauce. (It's her own recipe, and it's delicious!) Second, we buy skulls that are made of milk or dark chocolate. I don't like chocolate milkshakes. I like to keep them on the kitchen table for a few days before eating them. They look really cool!

2 **Write in your notebook.** Write about a custom or a special celebration when people use chocolate. Make sure all the sentences are related to the topic.

Unit 8

Cool Vacations!

VOCABULARY 1

1 **Look and write.** Use the words below to complete the sentences for each photo.

beach	camping	hotel	photo safari	relax	ruins
tent	theme park	tickets	tour	wildlife	

1. You can __________ by the pool at the __________.

2. They are __________. They are sitting in a __________.

3. They are taking a __________ of the __________.

4. They are buying __________ for a __________.

5. They can see ____________ on a ____________.

6. They are running on the ____________.

2 **Rank the vacations.** Write a sentence to say why you like or do not like each vacation.

camping	on a photo safari	see ruins	to a theme park

1. First, I want to go ________________________ because ________________________
____.

2. Second, I want to go ________________________ because ________________________
____.

3. Third, I want to go ________________________ because ________________________
____.

4. Fourth, I want to go ________________________ because ________________________
____.

GRAMMAR 1

Second conditional

If							
If	I	**lived**	near a beach,	I	**would go**	swimming every day.	*I'd* = *I would*
	he	**had**	money,	he	**would buy**	a new bike.	
	I	**were**	rich,	I	**'d travel**	around the world.	*he'd* = *he would*
	he	**didn't have**	homework,	he	**'d play**	video games.	

Real situation: *I don't live near the beach, so I can't go swimming every day.*
Imagined situation: *If I **lived** near a beach, I **would go** swimming every day.*
With *were*: *If I/you/he/she/we/they **were** rich . . .*

1 Read and underline the answer.

I like to take photos when I'm on vacation. If I *went* / *would go* on a photo safari, I *took* / *would take* photos of zebras. If we *saw* / *would see* lions, I *don't want* / *wouldn't want* to get too close. If the lions *came* / *would come* near the car, I *was* / *would be* afraid. I *liked* / *would like* it better if they *were* / *would be* giraffes. Giraffes have long necks and tongues. If I *saw* / *would see* a giraffe, I *took* / *would take* lots of photos. I *showed* / *would show* them to you if you *came* / *would come* to my house. If you *wanted* / *would want* to take one home with you, I *was* / *would be* happy to give one to you!

2 **Read.** Complete the sentences.

1. If I went (*go*) on a photo safari, I would see (*see*) wildlife.
2. They __________ (*go*) to a theme park if they __________ (*have*) tickets.
3. He __________ (*not go*) to the beach if he __________ (*have*) homework.
4. She __________ (*have*) a guide with her if she __________ (*go*) on a tour.
5. I __________ (*visit*) the ruins if I __________ (*go*) to Egypt.

3 **Read and write.** Complete the sentences.

1. If the theme park were open, I would buy an ice cream cone. (*buy*)
2. I would sleep outside __________. (*have*)
3. If you liked wildlife, __________. (*go*)
4. She would take a ship __________. (*go*)
5. If I went to the beach, __________. (*swim*)

VOCABULARY 2

1 Look and label.

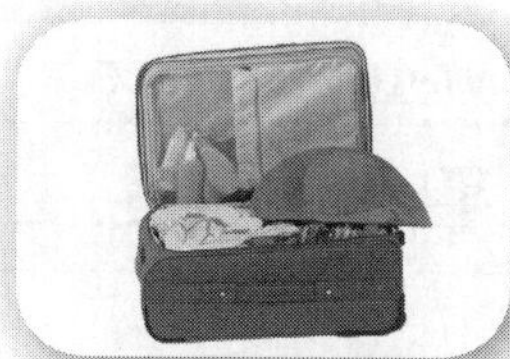

2 Read and write. Use the words from Activity 1.

1. My mom wears ______________ when it's sunny outside.
2. The screen at the ______________ showed the time that planes would arrive.
3. My brother has a ______________ with wheels to make it easy to carry.
4. My sister bought a ______________ so that she would remember our vacation.
5. My dad showed his ______________ at the airport when we returned to our country.

3 Listen and answer the questions. TR: 8.1

1. Where did Aunt Frida take the family?
2. What did Rosa's dad show at the airport?
3. What did Rosa get on vacation?
4. What did Julio get on vacation?
5. What did Julio think he left on vacation?
6. What was Rosa's surprise?

GRAMMAR 2

Would rather

I'd rather	watch a movie	**than**	play a video game.	*I'd = I would*
He**'d rather**	go swimming		(go) hiking.	*He'd = He would*

Question				**Answer**
Would you **rather**	go on a trip	**or**	stay home?	I'd rather go on a trip.
Would he **rather**	visit England		(visit) Australia?	He'd rather visit Australia.

When the verbs are the same, we don't usually say the second verb.
I'd rather go swimming than hiking. Would he rather visit England or Australia?

1 Read and write.

1. I / go to the movies / go to a baseball game

   I would rather go to the movies than (go to) a baseball game.

2. They / go swimming in a pool / go swimming in a lake

   ____

3. We / visit a museum / go to a concert

   ____

2 Complete the sentences.

1. She 'd rather eat breakfast than go to school hungry. (*breakfast / hungry*)
2. They ______________________. (*home / vacation*)
3. She ______________________. (*city / small town*)
4. He ______________________. (*music / film*)

3 **Write.** Rewrite your answers to Activity 2 as questions.

1. Would she rather eat breakfast or go to school hungry?
2. ______________________
3. ______________________
4. ______________________

SONG

1 **Listen to the song.** Fill in the missing words to complete the song. **TR: 8.2**

beach	camping	hiking	hotel	photos
relax	tour	vacation	wildlife	

If we went on a ______________,
we would see ______________.
I would take lots of ______________.
Wouldn't that be so nice?

I would like to stay at a ______________.
You'd like to ______________.

______________ and ______________!
The ______________ and the sun!
If we went on ______________,
it would be so much fun!

2 **Listen and repeat.** Which words rhyme with **more**? Which words rhyme with **hour**? Write. **TR: 8.3**

bore	pour	tower
floor	power	your
flower	shower	
our	sure	

more	hour

READING

1 **Listen and read.** TR: 8.4

The Forbidden City

The Forbidden City in Beijing, China, was built more than 600 years ago for the emperor of China. Construction began in 1406. It was completed 14 years later. Over the years, fires destroyed some buildings, but they were rebuilt each time. The main building was burned by fires in 1557 and 1597. After a battle in 1644, a bigger fire burned buildings in the city.

For 500 years, the Forbidden City was the home of 24 emperors. No one could enter the city without the emperor's invitation. The city is surrounded by a wall 10 meters high and a river 6 meters deep. The walls and river protected the emperor from outsiders.

The Forbidden City was first opened to the public as a museum in 1925. In 1987, it was made a World Heritage Site. Today, tourists can visit many of the buildings and see some of the emperors' treasures. Millions of people visit the city that was forbidden for hundreds of years!

2 **Check T for *True* and F for *False*.**

1. The Forbidden City was built for tourists. (T) (F)
2. The Forbidden City was built in 1925. (T) (F)
3. The Forbidden City is now a museum. (T) (F)
4. The Forbidden City is surrounded by a tall wall. (T) (F)

3 **Write.** Complete the time line. Use information from the reading.

Building begins.

1406 — 1420 — 1557 — 1597 — 1644 — 1925 — 1987

WRITING

Travel Review

A travel review describes someone's experience of a vacation. Based on your review, another person can decide if they want to do the same vacation. To make your writing interesting, you can use different kinds of sentences. You can use short, simple sentences to describe your ideas. Or you can combine your ideas into longer sentences. You can also use questions or exclamations.

1 **Read.** Read the ecotour review. Underline an example of a sentence that describes just one idea, and circle another that describes more than one idea.

Review of the Antigua Ecotour

If you wanted a special vacation on a beautiful island, where would you go? I recommend this ecotour in Antigua.

The tour guides took our small group on a boat to a natural rock bridge called Hell's Gate. We had to swim to the island and walk up the rocks and through a cave. Then we walked across the bridge. The view from the top was spectacular! The guides give you a tasty lunch on the boat and then it's time to go snorkeling! The boat stopped at a coral reef and we explored the wildlife. We saw many colorful fish. We saw a stingray, too! The water can be rough, so snorkeling is hard work. But it's worth the effort. When we got back on the boat, there was a snack of banana bread ready for us. Delicious!

If you prefer doing something active on vacation instead of sitting on the beach, this is the trip for you!

coral reef

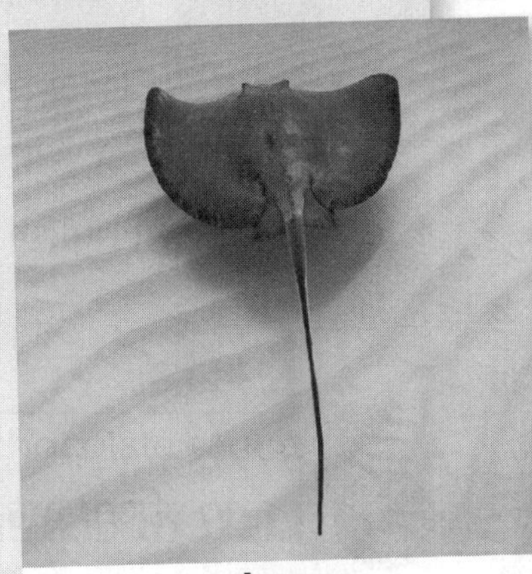
stingray

2 **Write in your notebook.** Write a review of a vacation. Tell what you liked and didn't like. Describe what you saw and did. Remember to use different types of sentences.

Review: Units 5–8

1 **Read and underline the correct words.** Then listen and check your answers. **TR: 8.5**

1. I've known my best friend *for* / *since* ten years!
2. Our parents have been friends *for* / *since* about twenty years.
3. We've studied at the same school *for* / *since* we were six years old.
4. We've spent our vacations together *for* / *since* 2012.
5. We used to fight a lot, but we haven't fought *for* / *since* a long time!

2 **Write in your notebook.** Answer the questions. Write two sentences. Use *for* and *since*. Use the words in each word bank.

How long have you done the activity? How much do you like doing the activity?

go camping	extremely
go skiing	incredibly
go to theme parks	really
live in your house	so
ride a bicycle	very
study English	

I've studied English for five years. I think it's really interesting!

3 **Listen.** Listen to Martha talk about the project. Who did what? Draw lines. **TR: 8.6**

Soldiers	Alex
Artifacts	Ben
Text	Martha
Photo	Suzy
Horse	

4 Write questions.

1. "These statues of soldiers are awesome!" they / make / Ben?
   Were they made by Ben?
2. "What about the artifacts?" they / paint / Alex?
3. "The text is very good." it / write / Suzy?
4. "I love the photo." it / take / the teacher?
5. "What about the horse?" it / buy or make / Martha?

5 **What about you?** Write a short paragraph. Use some of the words below.

Where in the world would you really like to visit? Why? What can you see and do there?

artifact	beach	camping	discover	equipment
photo safari	site	statue	theme park	treasure

6 **Read the descriptions of some words from Units 5-8.** What is the word for each one? The first letter is already there. There is one space for each other letter in the word.

1. This protects your head from injury.

   h _ _ _ _ _

2. This is a delicious, dark brown spice.

   c _ _ _ _ _ _ _ _

3. This is a place where a dead person is buried.

   t _ _ _

4. This is someone who takes something that does not belong to them.

   t _ _ _ _

5. You can make this with milk, ice cream, and cocoa powder.

   m _ _ _ _ _ _ _ _ _

6. This is a type of vacation where you can see animals in the wild.

   p _ _ _ _ s _ _ _ _ _

7 **Listen and write.** Complete the chart. **TR: 8.7**

1

2

3

4

What was happening in the picture?	Why?
1. The boy was wearing a huge hat	so that he wouldn't get sunburned.
2. He was carrying a big map	so that
3. He	so that he could learn how it is made.
4. She	so that

8 **Read.** Check T for *True* and F for *False*.

If you like warm weather, sandy beaches, and lots of fun things to do, you will like Dubai! Dubai is a great place to go on vacation! It is on the Arabian Peninsula. A *peninsula* is land that stretches into the water like a big toe. Dubai is a very modern place. You can stay at a hotel on a man-made island. If you visit Dubai, you will see one of the tallest buildings in the world. It's over 800 meters (2,625 feet) tall! If you would rather go to a theme park, there are many choices. At one theme park, activities about nature, culture, science, and space can be found. You can play a game that is like flying a real airplane at this theme park.

You can also see Dubai from the air in a hot-air balloon. If you would rather ride a camel in the desert, you can! Because of the warm weather, it doesn't snow in Dubai, but you can still play in the snow inside a shopping mall. There is man-made snow and a mountain. If you would rather go in the water, a water park is nearby. There is even a park where you can swim with dolphins! If you go to Dubai, you will have a lot of fun!

1. Dubai is a modern place. (T) (F)
2. A hotel can be found on a man-made island. (T) (F)
3. If you went to Dubai, you would not find any theme parks. (T) (F)
4. If you like snow, you will find it in a shopping mall in Dubai. (T) (F)
5. You cannot ride a camel in Dubai. (T) (F)

9 **Read.** Complete the sentences

1. If I ______________ (*see*) a souvenir I liked, I ______________ (*buy*) it.
2. They ________________ (*rather listen*) to a concert than go to a movie.
3. If she ______________ (*have*) a dog, she ______________ (*take*) it for a walk.
4. We ______________ (*play*) basketball if we ______________ (*have*) a ball.
5. You ________________ (*rather sleep*) a little longer.
6. She ______________________ (*rather go camping*) than visit the beach.

EXPLORE OUR WORLD

TR: 9.1

This is our world.
Everybody's got a song to sing.
Each boy and girl.
This is our world!

I say, "Our." You say, "World."
Our!
World!
Our!
World!

I say, "Boy." You say, "Girl."
Boy!
Girl!
Boy!
Girl!

I say, "Everybody move!"
I say, "Everybody stop!"
Everybody stop!

This is our world.
Everybody's got a song to sing.
Each boy and girl.
This is our world!

UNIT 1 KEEP YOUR CULTURE STRONG Song 1

Knowing your history is important.
Holding on to your culture is an excellent thing!
Knowing your history is important.
It's up to you to keep your culture strong!

What special art does your culture bring to our world?

What special thing does your family bring to our world?

Weaving? Learn to do it!

Storytelling? Learn to tell it!

What brings your culture pride?

CHORUS

What special art does your culture bring to our world?

What special thing does your family bring to our world?

Embroidery? Learn to sew it!

Sculpture? Learn to sculpt it!

What brings your culture pride?

Your grandparents may seem old to you,

but they know a thing or two!

CHORUS

UNIT 2 PLANTS ARE ALL AROUND Song 2

Leaf and stem and flower and root!
The sweet, delicious smell of fruit
is here and there and everywhere!
Plants are all around.

Plants are growing
up and down.
Air is flowing
all around.

Plants come in every shape and size.
Their bright colors attract the eyes
of bees and butterflies.

Big and small,
plants survive it all.

CHORUS

Some plants play tricks with our eyes.
They're made to give us a surprise.
A plant is designed to survive.
To make new seeds, to grow and thrive.

Some of the oldest plants on Earth
are trees on mountains high,
drinking in the light,
reaching up into the sky.

Leaf and stem and flower and root!
The sweet, delicious smell of fruit
is here and there and everywhere!
Plants are all around.

UNIT 3 VOLCANOES ARE A LOT LIKE ME Song 3

Volcanoes are a lot like me.
Some are awake and full of energy.
Other volcanoes are sleeping.
Yes, volcanoes are a lot like me!

When I get really silly,
and my energy builds up,
if it has no place to go,
sometimes I think I will explode!

Deep inside a volcano,
heat and gas are building up.
If they have no place to go,
the volcano will erupt!

CHORUS

If a volcano is dormant,
it's really just asleep.
A dormant volcano will sleep for centuries.

If a volcano is active,
it's very wide awake.
When it's awake, it's just like me.
It's ready to blow off some energy!

CHORUS

UNIT 4 THE THREE Rs Song 4

When you're walking to the trash can
with some old stuff in your hand,
you might want to stop and think again.
Can this be reused or given away?
Let's start taking care of our world today!

Reduce. Reuse. Recycle.
Do it every day.
Don't throw everything into the trash
when clearly there's another way.

Reduce. Reuse. Recycle.
Help keep our world clean.
Do your part every day
to make our world green!

Recycling is easy when you know what to do.
Glass? Paper? Metal?
These things can be reused,
again, and again, and again!

CHORUS

Compost your uneaten food.
Composting isn't hard to do.
Natural things can be reused
when they get a helping hand from you!

Reduce. Reuse. Recycle.
Do it every day.
Don't throw everything into the trash
when clearly there's another way.

Reduce. Reuse. Recycle.
Help keep our world clean.
Reduce. Reuse. Recycle.
Help make our world green!

UNIT 5 EXTREME SPORTS Song 5

A kitesurfer rides the waves.
A kitesurfer rides the wind.
I've kitesurfed in my dreams
ever since I was a kid!

Extreme sports.
Flying high in the air!
Other sports
don't compare!

Extreme sports.
Look around.
They're everywhere!

Super cool sports!

Skiers flip so skillfully,
incredibly high above the snow.
I've skied in my dreams
ever since I was a kid.

CHORUS

Extreme sports.
Look around.
They're everywhere!

Super cool sports!

Motocross and hang-gliding,
are so incredibly fun!
I've dreamed of doing both
ever since I was a kid!

CHORUS

Extreme sports.
Look around.
They're everywhere!
Super cool sports!

UNIT 6 SO MUCH TO LEARN Song 6

History's a mystery,
and that's why I like history!
Buried statues and mummies, too!
So much to learn.
So much to do!

Excavated kings
were found by archaeologists.
Anglo Saxon treasure
was discovered
in the mist.

The Terra-cotta Army
was found deep underground.
Just think what you might find
if you look around.

CHORUS

Objects that were hidden
can be found by scientists.
Pottery and paper,
gold and money,
in the mist.

If we learn from history,
wisdom from the past
can help us answer questions
we really want to ask.

CHORUS

History's a mystery,
and that's why I like history!
Buried statues and mummies, too!
So much to learn.
So much to do!

UNIT 7 HOT CHOCOLATE Song 7

Hey! Do you like hot chocolate?

Put some chocolate in a cup.
Get some milk and heat it up.
Stir in some vanilla. Add some spice.
Sprinkle on some cinnamon.

It'll taste right!

I was making hot chocolate
in the kitchen one night.
My grandma was telling me
I wasn't doing it right.

She was telling me about her mother.
About how she made cocoa when she was young.
She was telling me to sit down,
when she said, "I'm going to show you how it's done."

CHORUS

Hot chocolate in a cup.
Hot chocolate! Pour it to the top.
Hot chocolate tastes so good.
I learned to make it like Grandma said I should.

I love hot chocolate!

CHORUS

Hot chocolate in a cup.
Hot chocolate! Pour it to the top.
Hot chocolate tastes so good.
I learned to make it like Grandma said I should!

Hot chocolate!

UNIT 8 IF I WENT ON VACATION Song 8

Let's go on vacation!
Let's go on a trip!

If we went on vacation,
we would take a big ship
across the ocean,
far, far away.

If I had my way,
I would go today!

Camping and hiking!
The beach and the sun!
If we went on vacation,
it would be so much fun!

If we went on a tour,
we would see wildlife.
I would take lots of photos.
Wouldn't that be so nice?

CHORUS

I would like to stay at a hotel.
You'd like to relax.

Camping and hiking!
The beach and the sun!
If we went on vacation,
it would be so much fun!

If I weren't afraid of heights,
we could climb a mountain.
But I am! So let's go to the water park
and take pictures by the fountain.

CHORUS